AGNEW'S

1982-1992

JAN GOSSAERT CALLED MABUSE (died c. 1533)

Portrait of a Young Man, oil on panel, 15 x 11 inches (38 x 28 cm.)

Private collection, 1984

AGNEW'S
1982-1992

CONTRIBUTORS

Julian Agnew

William Agnew

Christopher Drake

Magdalen Evans

Evelyn Joll

Dick Kingzett

Rodney Merrington

Gabriel Naughton

William Plomer

Susan Williams

Andrew Wyld

ENDEAVOUR

LONDON

Agnew's would like to make the following additional acknowledgements:

Plate 31

Purchase, The Annenburg Foundation, Mrs Charles Wrightsman,
Michel David-Weill, The Dillon Fund, Henry J and Drue Heinz Foundation,
Lola Kramarsky, Annette de la Renta, Mr and Mrs Arthur Ochs Sulzberger,
The Vincent Astor Foundation and the Peter Jay Sharp Foundation Gifts;
The Lesley and Emma Sheafer Collection, Bequest of Emma A Sheafer, and
Theodore M Davis Collection, Bequest of Theodore M Davis, by exchange;
Gift of George R Hahn, in memory of his mother, Annie Sykes Hann, by
exchange; Gifts of George A Hearn, George Blumenthal, George H and
Helen M Richard and Mrs George A Stern and Bequests of Helen Hay Whitney
and John Henry Abegg and Anonymous Bequest, by exchange; supplemented by
gifts and funds from the friends of the Museum, 1990 (1990.196)

Plate 43

Gift of Nancy Hamon in memory of Jake L Hamon with additional donations from
Mrs Eugene D McDermott, Mrs James H Clark, Mrs Edwards Marcus and the
Leyland Fikes Foundation Inc.

Plates 138 and *157*

Restricted gifts of Dr William D Shorey (*Plate 138* in memory of Sarah R Shorey;
Olivia Shaler Swan Fund, 1988.513). Photographs © 1991. The Art Institute of
Chicago. All rights reserved.

Plate 189

Purchase, The Edith Perry Chapman Fund and Bequest of Bernard M. Baruch,
by exchange.

Front Cover

Joseph Wright of Derby *Mr and Mrs Coltman about to set out on a Ride* (detail)
see Plate 14.

Produced by
Endeavour Group, UK. 85 Larkhall Rise, London, SW4 6HR

Designed by Paul Welti
Edited by Kate Oldfield

ISBN 1 873913 02 8

Typeset by The R & B Partnership
Printed in Hong Kong by IMAGO

CONTENTS

INTRODUCTION

THIS IS THE THIRD BOOK TO CHRONICLE the history and achievements of Agnew's. The firm became 175 years old in 1992 and this volume deals solely with the decade 1982-1992, which happens to correspond exactly with my time as chairman, although, by the time this book appears, I will have been succeeded by Julian Agnew.

This volume differs quite markedly in format from its predecessor: *A Dealer's Record: Agnew's 1967-81*. In that case there were ten essays by specialist scholars on individual pictures of particular importance and these were supplemented by a wide selection of photographs of items in all categories sold during the period. These photographs bore captions merely giving artist, title, size, buyer's name and year of sale, although some were also mentioned briefly in Julian Agnew's introduction which also surveyed the art market in general. In this book all the items chosen for illustration will be described in a way that we hope readers will find interesting, and all departments in the firm will give an account of their activities. This means that the explanatory role of the introduction, so necessary in *A Dealer's Record*, is no longer required. Instead, I aim to give some account of past matters not covered elsewhere in the book, together with a brief mention of our plans for the future.

1981 had been our least successful year for a long time, but things improved considerably in 1982 and from then until the middle of 1990 the pattern was of steady expansion and continuing success, a story doubtless parallelled by hundreds if not thousands of firms in Thatcherite Britain. Although inflation persist-

ed, borrowing money was positively encouraged, and boom conditions existed in the art market with prices rising steadily and records being broken almost weekly. It was certainly a bumper time for the auctioneers who made sure that their successes received extensive coverage in the Press. It became fashionable, especially in New York, to be seen at the major sales, although these became less entertaining when the paddle system of bidding was introduced. This meant that a successful bidder, instead of giving his name to the auctioneers, held up an object like a ping-pong bat with a number on it, thus remaining anonymous. And if anonymity was the goal, a battery of telephones installed in the saleroom enabled buyers to bid from anywhere in the world. Although a battle between 'the white telephone and the black telephone' might be music to the vendor's ears, it became unbearably tedious and drawn-out for everyone else. Yet it is undeniable that more and more owners were attracted to auction when they wished to sell, to the detriment of dealers who had always hitherto been offered privately a good share of the best things to come onto the market. The auction boom finally reached its apogee when Mr Saito, chairman of a Japanese paper manufacturing company, bought within three days in May 1990 in New York a van Gogh and a Renoir for a total of $160m.

Prices for contemporary art were perhaps even more extraordinary, Jasper Johns' *Two Flags* fetching $11m and Willem de Kooning's *Interchange* $18,800,000 on 8 November 1989. The sterling equivalent of the latter, £11,898,735, was thus more than five times as much as that which Velasquez' *Portrait of Juan de*

Room 32 at the National Gallery
(by courtesy of the National Gallery, London)

Pareja had brought in 1970 (£2,310,000) which was more than twice the amount any picture had previously fetched at auction.

But during the second half of 1990 and throughout 1991 the auction bubble burst and saleroom correspondents no longer chronicled successes but wrote instead of 'disasters' and even 'carnage'. This resulted in more pictures being offered once again by private owners to dealers, a situation which was further fuelled by the growing recession and by the considerable losses suffered by some members of Lloyds.

From 1987 onwards, for the first time, the number of executive directors not related to the Agnew family equalled that of family members. During this period many changes took place at Agnew's. In 1983 almost the entire building was redecorated when the crimson wall coverings of Genoese velvet, which had been in place since about 1900, became too dilapidated and were replaced with new material. A computer was installed under the expert guidance of Mark

Robertson who succeeded Frank Potter as Company Secretary in 1984. Much more recently the accounts department has been moved downstairs to make space both for a new watercolour gallery and a room in which to display sculpture. Redecoration did not end in Bond Street, for we also undertook to pay for the refurbishment and restoration of Room 32 in the National Gallery, the largest in the building, at a cost of £360,000. The room was reopened to the public on 27 March 1991 and we held a celebratory reception there on 11 June which was voted a great success.

In May 1986 we acquired a presence in New York, after an interval of nearly 60 years, by renting an apartment near the Museum of Modern Art which serves as a base for visiting members of the firm. This has helped greatly to stimulate our business in America and we have also found that a base in New York is of value in increasing our business with Japanese clients, which has proved so important recently as is recorded elsewhere in this book.

One important activity at Agnew's, not mentioned in *A Dealer's Record*, concerns our loan exhibitions held in aid of charity. These continue a tradition which goes back at least to the early years of this century. Although these exhibitions take a considerable amount of time and effort and are expensive to arrange, we feel that they are very worthwhile in fulfilling the dual purpose of raising money for the causes concerned and by giving pleasure to those who visit them. Therefore I hope it will be of interest to list in chronological order those held during this period. As will be seen the list includes collections normally difficult of access: *Thomas Holloway: The Benevolent Millionaire*. Pictures from Royal Holloway College in aid of The Victorian Society. *Treasures from Dulwich* in aid of the Dulwich Picture Gallery Appeal. *Thirty-five Paintings from the Collection of the British Rail Pension Fund* in aid of the British Diabetic Association.

German Impressionism and Expressionism from Leicester in aid of the Friends of the Leicester Museum Fund. *The Marquess of Cholmondeley's Collection of Military Pictures, Drawings and Prints* in aid of the Soldiers', Sailors' and Airmen's Families Association and the Artists' General Benevolent Institution. *The Treasures of Fyvie* in aid of the National Trust for Scotland. *Watercolours from the Whitworth Art Gallery, University of Manchester* in aid of the Gallery's Centenary Appeal for an extension to the Gallery.

In addition, Agnew's have been hosts on three occasions to the National Trust Foundation for Art, an organisation formed in 1986 under the chairmanship of Sir Brinsley Ford in order to enrich National Trust properties with pictures and sculpture by contemporary artists with especial emphasis on young artists of promise. Two exhibitions and an auction have been held, the latter raising over £100,000 for the project, in December 1989.

We have also staged two concerts of chamber music in the top gallery, one in aid of the N.A.C.F. and the second in aid of the Courtauld Institute, and we plan further concerts in support of other causes in the future.

As will be seen from the chapters which follow, several departments have grown considerably in the past decade: sculpture, which only started when William Agnew joined the firm in 1979, and prints, which expanded greatly after Christopher Drake joined Agnew's in 1988. He took over from Bill Plomer, who retired in 1990 after 37 years during which he made many friends both for himself and for Agnew's. The British paintings of the 20th century and Contemporary art departments have also grown steadily, and, in spite of William Joll's resignation at the end of 1991, we intend to continue our activities in these areas.

One new venture has been our participation in a number of art fairs: in 1989 we made a highly successful re-entry into Grosvenor House

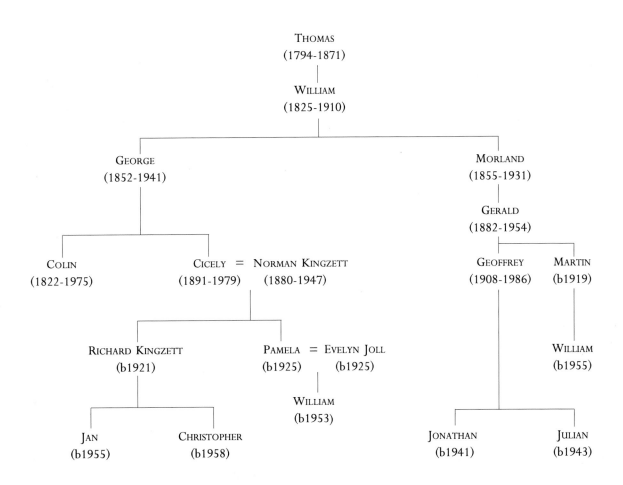

THOMAS
(1794-1871)

WILLIAM
(1825-1910)

GEORGE
(1852-1941)

MORLAND
(1855-1931)

GERALD
(1882-1954)

COLIN
(1822-1975)

CICELY = NORMAN KINGZETT
(1891-1979)   (1880-1947)

GEOFFREY
(1908-1986)

MARTIN
(b1919)

RICHARD KINGZETT
(b1921)

PAMELA = EVELYN JOLL
(b1925)   (b1925)

WILLIAM
(b1955)

WILLIAM
(b1953)

JAN
(b1955)

CHRISTOPHER
(b1958)

JONATHAN
(b1941)

JULIAN
(b1943)

Six generations in a family firm.

after an interval of 30 years and we have also aimed at attracting new European clients by going to the Paris *Biennale* and to Palazzo Strozzi in Florence, with encouraging results. Although all fairs last too long in the opinion of the exhibitors, so far they seem powerless to reduce the length. But we certainly mean to persevere with them and even have other fairs in mind as possibilities for the future.

At the time of writing, it is difficult to predict what effect '1993' will have on the art market in Europe. Negotiations over the harmonisation of V.A.T. in the community have not yet been concluded, but an unsatisfactory result would be a major blow to London's status as a centre for the market.

Although works of art should be allowed to move freely between countries in the E.E.C.,

there may well be some countries that still impose stringent controls on indigenous works of art. In this context Spain and Italy at once come to mind. In Britain our export system, which has worked so well since the War has recently become seriously underfunded and now needs more support. At present, however, London's leading position in the art market, although already supplanted in some areas, is still intact in the field of Old Masters, and Britain thus remains potentially the most rewarding country for Old Master dealers.

Whatever the future may hold, we shall endeavour to ensure that the firm maintains its position as one of the pre-eminent international art dealers well into the 21st century.

EVELYN JOLL

Chapter 1

MUSEUMS IN THE UNITED KINGDOM

THE DECADE 1982-1992 WAS ONE OF great difficulty for U.K. museums. This was due to a concatenation of circumstances: the steep rise in prices for works of art during the 1980s while inflation steadily eroded the purchasing power of the pound. To cope with these two factors museums would have needed massive increases in their funds but instead grants remained woefully inadequate: few were raised, many were frozen (since the fiscal year 1985-6 the National Museums' grants have remained the same) while others were actually reduced or, in the case of rate-capped councils, withdrawn altogether. Nothing highlights the plight of U.K. museums more than the single statistic that the price fetched at auction in May 1990 by van Gogh's portrait of *Doctor Gachet*, $82.5 million or £43,107,142, was three times the annual purchasing grants of all the national museums and galleries put together.

In spite of this museums managed to make some notably distinguished acquisitions during this period. In order to do so, much financial assistance was required from bodies such as the National Heritage Memorial Fund, the National Art Collections Fund, the Victoria and Albert Museum Fund and the Pilgrim Trust as well as from public and private donors.

Taking the acquisitions school by school, and, within them, in chronological order, the earliest pictures are the two Cranach panels (Plates 1a and 1b), already on loan to the National Gallery from the Loyd Collection, on whose behalf we negotiated a private treaty sale to the gallery in 1987. These pictures formed the shutters of Cranach's *St. Catherine Altarpiece*, now in the Dresden Gallery. The centre panel, which depicts the martyrdom of the Saint, is dated 1506. The Loyd panels were sold by Dresden in 1797. In the left shutter St. Christina is shown standing on the millstone which miraculously floated when, tied to it, she was thrown into the lake of Bolsena. St. Ottila of Alsace holds the book of Rules of the Benedictine Order. On the book are a pair of eyes, a reference to the cure of her blindness. In the right shutter St. Geneviève of Paris holds the candle which, extinguished by the wind, miraculously relit when she picked it up. St. Apollonia holds a tooth in a pair of pincers, a reference to the brutal way in which she was martyred.

The finest picture belonging to the late Mark Oliver (1896 - 1987), a collector and owner of the Savile Gallery, was El Greco's *Fábula*. Due to his friendship with Colin Thompson, director of the National Gallery of Scotland from 1977 - 1984, Mark Oliver directed in his will that Edinburgh should be given the first option to acquire the El Greco. On behalf of the Oliver executors Agnew's supplied a valuation of the picture which was accepted as the basis for the successful negotiations which followed. To celebrate the acquisition the National Gallery of Scotland put on an exhibition in the late summer of 1989, *El Greco : Mystery and Illumination* at which the Oliver picture - now retitled

Plate 1a

LUCAS CRANACH THE ELDER

1472 - 1553

St. Christina and St. Ottila

(from the *St. Catherine Altarpiece*)

Oil on panel, 47½ x 24¾ inches (120.7 x 63 cm.)

The National Gallery, London, 1987.

Reproduced by courtesy of the Trustees.

Plate 1b

LUCAS CRANACH THE ELDER

1472 - 1553

St. Geneviève and St. Apollonia

(from the *St. Catherine Altarpiece*)

Oil on panel, 47½ x 24¾ inches (120.7 x 63 cm.)

The National Gallery, London, 1987.

Reproduced by courtesy of the Trustees.

Allegory (Plate 2) and dated c.1585 - was shown together with the version belonging to Lord Harewood, and other relevant paintings by El Greco and comparable candlelight pictures by artists such as Lievens and Rubens. The precise meaning of the picture remains elusive, although some ingenious theories were put forward in the excellent catalogue of the exhibition.

The handsome Alessandro Allori (1535 - 1607) *Portrait of a Young Man*, (Plate 3) dated 1590, was sold at the Mentmore sale in 1977 where we underbid it. However, the picture was refused an export licence later that year so the owner decided to lend it to the Ashmolean. In 1982 the Allori was again sent to Sotheby's where we bought it for the Ashmolean, a happy outcome and one of the major acquisitions made towards the end of David Piper's directorship as he retired in 1985.

In the 1884 catalogue of the Mentmore pictures the portrait was assigned to Bronzino and described as representing Benvenuto Cellini. This identification was undoubtedly wrong but the portrait is of such high quality that it is easy to understand how Bronzino's name came to be attached to it.

Nearly 100 years later than the Allori portrait, Giovanni Battista Gaulli (1639 - 1709), usually known as Baciccio, painted Cardinal Marco Gallo's portrait (Plate 4) which we sold to the National Gallery in March, 1991. This was the first painting by Baciccio to enter the Gallery's collection which was weak in Roman portraiture of this period.

Although born in Genoa, Baciccio spent his working life in Rome where he is chiefly renowned for having painted the immense ceiling of the Jesuit church, the Gesù, between 1676 and 1679. He is also recorded as having painted 'innumerable' portraits: few of these, however, are known today and still fewer are in Britain. Marco Gallo, appointed Bishop of

Rimini in 1659, was made a Cardinal on 1 September 1681 and died of apoplexy on 24 July 1683. This portrait, which shows the influence of Baciccio's mentor Bernini most notably in the sculptural handling of the drapery, must have been painted between these two dates.

By chance, all three 17th century Flemish pictures that we sold were painted within a span of four years. The earlier sketch by Rubens, *Aeneas in the Underworld*, (Plate 5) illustrates ll. 290-1 of the sixth book of the *Aeneid* when Aeneas, in search of his dead father, Anchises, imagines himself surrounded by terrifying creatures such as Gorgons, Harpies and the Hydra and gets ready to defend himself.

Professor Michael Jaffé proposes a date of 1630-31 while Professor Held prefers 1635-7.

We bought the sketch in New York in 1959 and sold it to Boyd Alexander, the biographer of William Beckford. After Boyd Alexander's death, we negotiated a private treaty sale on behalf of his nephew with the National Museum of Wales in December, 1984.

James I Uniting the Kingdoms of England and Scotland (Plate 6) is one of the five surviving sketches that Rubens made for *The Union of the Crowns*, one of the nine large paintings on the ceiling of the Banqueting House in Whitehall. These were finished in August 1634, therefore a date of c.1632-3 for the sketch seems most likely.

Professor Held points out that Rubens began with the guardsman as the King's robe is clearly painted around the soldier's outline. The two figures reappear in a much more highly developed sketch in the Hermitage, Leningrad.

Our sketch belonged to the artist Richard Cosway who sold it at auction in London in 1822. It was then bought by Colonel T.M. Davies, passing by descent to Lt-Col. H.R.H. Davies. On his death we negotiated a private treaty sale in 1984 on behalf of his executors with the City Art Gallery, Birmingham where

Plate 2
DOMENIKOS THEOTOKOPOLOUS, CALLED EL GRECO
1541-1614
Fábula
Oil on canvas, 26½ x 34⅞ inches (67.3 x 88.6 cm.)
The National Gallery of Scotland, 1989

Plate 3

ALESSANDRO ALLORI

1535-1607

Portrait of a Young Man

Oil on panel, 52⅜ x 41 inches (133 x 104.2 cm.)

The Ashmolean Museum, Oxford, 1982

Plate 4

GIOVANNI BATTISTA GAULLI KNOWN AS IL BACICCIO

1639-1709

Marco, Cardinal Gallo

Oil on canvas, 30 x 25 inches (76.2 x 63.5 cm.)

The National Gallery, London, 1991.

Reproduced by courtesy of the Trustees.

Plate 5

SIR PETER PAUL RUBENS

1577-1640

Aeneas in the Underworld

Oil on panel, 18½ x 12½ inches (47 x 38 cm.)

National Museum of Wales, 1984

Plate 6

SIR PETER PAUL RUBENS

1577-1640

James I Uniting the Kingdoms of England and Scotland

Oil on panel, 25 x 19⅛ inches (63.5 x 48.3 cm.)

Birmingham Museum and Art Gallery, 1984

Plate 7

Sir Anthony van Dyck

1599-1641

Venetia Stanley, Lady Digby as Prudence

Oil on canvas, 39¼ x 31½ inches (99.7 x 79.4 cm.)

The National Portrait Gallery, London, 1984

Plate 8

PIETER JANSZ SAENREDAM

1597-1665

The Interior of St. Bavo, Haarlem

Oil on oak panel, 68 x 56½ inches (174.8 x 143.6 cm.)

The National Gallery of Scotland, 1982

[19]

the sketch had previously been on loan for several years.

Van Dyck's portrait of *Venetia Stanley, Lady Digby as Prudence* (Plate 7) was commissioned soon after her death in 1633 by her grieving husband Sir Kenelm Digby, whom she had married against her mother's wishes, probably in 1626. She was a famous beauty and had been kept in her youth by the 3rd Earl of Dorset 'as his concubine'. Aubrey wrote a famous description of her looks and in particular on the colour of her cheeks - 'just that of the Damask rose, which is neither too hott nor too pale...'

The iconography of this allegorical portrait, ordered perhaps as a vindication of the sitter's reputation, is described by Oliver Millar in the catalogue of the exhibition *Van Dyck in England*, held at the National Portrait Gallery in 1982-3. The portrait was sold by Agnew's in 1965 to a private collector in Warwickshire on whose behalf we resold it to the National Portrait Gallery in 1984.

The two 17th century Dutch pictures by Saenredam and Cuyp that we sold during this period have three things in common: both belonged to the Marquess of Bute, each is the largest known painting by the artist in question and each is considered to be his masterpiece.

The Saenredam of *The Interior of St. Bavo, Haarlem* (Plate 8) has an inscription which states that it was finished on 27 February, 1648. Three months later Saenredam wrote to Constantin Huygens, who had seen the picture, in the hope of getting his help in selling it to the new Stadholder in the Hague, Prince William II. However nothing came of this and the picture was sold to an Amsterdam burgomaster from whose collection it was acquired by the State of Holland to give to Charles II as part of the so-called 'Dutch Gift'. It only remained in the English Royal Collection until early in the 18th century. In 1934 it was sold by the Neave family, and later bought in 1936 by the 4th

Marquess of Bute. The painting was then bought from his son's collection through Agnew's by the National Gallery of Scotland in 1982.

The Cuyp *Landscape with Horseman and Peasants* (Plate 9) probably dates from the late 1650s. It had entered the Bute collection by 1764 when it was engraved and was then even larger, about 10 inches having been removed at the top at some later date. It has been fairly described as 'the grandest of Cuyp's landscapes and certainly a pinnacle in the Dutch art of landscape'. According to Benjamin West it was this picture that encouraged so many English collectors to buy Cuyp's painting with the result that Britain is now far richer in his work than Holland.

The Bute Cuyp was bought through Agnew's by the National Gallery in 1989.

The three canvases by Boucher: *L'Offrande à la Villageoise* (1761), *La Jardinière Endormie* (1762) and *L'Aimable Pastorale* (1762) (Plates 10, 11 and 12) were all commissioned by the Maréchal de Saincy whose family were Boucher's most important patrons after Madame de Pompadour, to decorate his *hôtel* just off the Place des Victoires.

Sold in 1789, they passed into the Rothschild collection at Mentmore and thence by descent to Lord Rosebery at Mentmore whence they were sold in 1964 and bought by Agnew's for Mr Herbert Showering. After Mr Showering's death Agnew's sold them on behalf of his estate by private treaty to the National Gallery of Scotland in 1986. They now look, in the octagonal room at Edinburgh, as if they had been painted to hang there.

The Francis Cotes portrait of *The Astley Children* (Plate 13) is signed and dated 1767 and shows Anna Maria Astley, aged 7, and her brother, Edward, aged 5½. This seems to have been commissioned by their maternal grandfather, Christopher Milles, as it descended through the Milles family to the 4th Earl Sondes

Plate 9

AELBERT CUYP

1620-91

Landscape with Horseman and Peasants

Oil on canvas, 49 x 96 inches (124.5 x 244 cm.)

The National Gallery, London, 1989.

Reproduced by courtesy of the Trustees.

Plate 10
FRANÇOIS BOUCHER
1703-70
L'Offrande à la Villageoise
Oil on canvas, 90 x 35 inches (229 x 89 cm.)
The National Gallery of Scotland, 1986

Plate 11
FRANÇOIS BOUCHER
1703-70
La Jardinière Endormie
Oil on canvas, 90 x 35 inches (229 x 89 cm.)
The National Gallery of Scotland, 1986

Plate 12
FRANÇOIS BOUCHER
1703-70
L'Aimable Pastorale
Oil on canvas, 90 x 35 inches (229 x 89 cm.)
The National Gallery of Scotland, 1986

Plate 13

Francis Cotes R.A.

1726-70

Anna Maria Astley aged 7 and her brother
Edward aged 5¹/₂.

Oil on canvas, 78 ¾ x 63 ¾ inches (200 x 162 cm.)

The Tate Gallery, London, 1981

(d.1970). It was sold by his Trustees at Phillips on 11 November 1980 (lot 38), bought by Agnew's, from whom it was bought by the Tate Gallery in 1981, thus just too late for inclusion in the second volume of the firm's history published in that year.

The children grew up at Melton Constable in Norfolk. Their father, Sir Edward Astley, was MP for the county from 1768-90; he proposed, among other things, that there should be a tax on dogs, but perhaps the gigantic dog in Cotes' picture was no longer alive by then. The 1760s was the period when Cotes became a serious rival to Reynolds. One can understand why some patrons did not care for Reynolds' classical approach to portraiture, preferring Cotes' more informal treatment, seen here in this enchanting picture of two spirited children at its very best.

In 1771, four years after the Cotes was painted, Wright of Derby's portrait of *Mr and Mrs Coltman* (Plate 14) was almost certainly exhibited at the Society of Artists (as 'A small conversation'). The picture descended in the family until sold at Christie's on 23 November 1984 (lot 94) when Agnew's bought it on behalf of the National Gallery, their purchase being assisted with grants by the National Heritage Memorial Fund and the Pilgrim Trust.

In the catalogue of the Wright of Derby exhibition at the Tate in 1990, Judy Egerton wrote: 'Wright is not often a lyrical artist: but that is what he becomes with his matchless portrait of Thomas Coltman and his wife Mary'. And later she observes that the picture 'is more than just a highly successful double portrait; it is also one of the most affectionate portraits of a happy marriage in the whole of British art'.

One of Thomas Coltman's friends was the famous naturalist and explorer Sir Joseph Banks (1743-1820) whose portrait by Reynolds (Plate 15), exhibited at the Royal Academy in 1773, was bought through Agnew's from the collec-

tion at Parham Park by the National Portrait Gallery in 1986. Banks had accompanied Captain Cook on his voyage round the world from 1768-71 and was later to become President of the Royal Society, an office he held for 41 years. Reynolds' portrait, an undoubted masterpiece, shows him seated in his study in a relaxed and informal pose. But one is nevertheless made aware of the sitter's energy so that it is easy to believe that he was 'always in the first boat when landing on any new shore'.

During the 1980s the Fitzwilliam Museum acquired two important landscapes from us by John Sell Cotman (1987) and Richard Parkes Bonington (1983).

Boats at Anchor on Breydon Water (Plate 16) belongs to the period 1806-1810, the years in the early part of Cotman's career when he gave some attention to oil painting, a practice he then abandoned for a decade or so. The picture reveals in the painting of the boats the same sense of form and structure that one finds in the 'Greta Bridge' period watercolours. At the same time the calm reflections in the water and the feeling of distance between the boats and the shore imbue the composition with a sense of tranquillity that is entirely satisfying.

In contrast the little Bonington panel sparkles with sunlight. The picture belonged originally to the poet and collector Samuel Rogers and was traditionally entitled *Lake Garda*. This is, however, incorrect and Patrick Noon, in the 1991-2 Bonington Exhibition catalogue, identified the scene as *Boccadasse with Monte Fascia in the Distance*, (Plate 17), Boccadasse being a suburb of Genoa. The view would have been sketched by Bonington on his way from Spezia to Genoa with Baron Rivet in early June, 1826. As Noon writes, 'this atmospheric study of the Appenines unites studied observation and concise execution, a combination typical of the Italian oils yet rarely as felicitous as here.'

Although Constable must have begun work

Plate 14

JOSEPH WRIGHT OF DERBY A.R.A.

1734-97

Mr and Mrs Coltman about to set out on a Ride

Oil on canvas, 50 x 40 inches (127 x 101.8 cm.)

The National Gallery, London, 1984.

Reproduced by courtesy of the Trustees.

Plate 15

SIR JOSHUA REYNOLDS P.R.A.

1723-92

Sir Joseph Banks

Oil on canvas, 50 x 40 inches (127 x 101.8 cm.)

The National Portrait Gallery, London, 1986

Plate 16 (above)

JOHN SELL COTMAN

1782-1842

Boats at Anchor on Breydon Water

Oil on canvas, 20 x 29 inches (51 x 74.7 cm.)

The Fitzwilliam Museum, 1988.

Reproduced by the permission of the Syndics.

Plate 17 (below)

RICHARD PARKES BONINGTON

1802-28

Boccadasse with Monte Fascia in the Distance

Oil on board, 10 x 13 inches (25.5 x 33 cm.)

The Fitzwilliam Museum, 1983.

Reproduced by the permission of the Syndics.

on *The Opening of Waterloo Bridge* (Plate 18) before Bonington painted his Italian view in 1826, the picture was not exhibited at the Royal Academy until 1832. It commemorates the ceremony which took place on 18 June 1817, the second anniversary of the Battle of Waterloo.

The preliminary sketches dating back to 1819, the other version now at Anglesey Abbey, and the tribulations that beset Constable when painting this picture, are all described in full in the catalogue of the Constable exhibition held at the Tate in 1991. In the exhibited picture Constable adopted a higher viewpoint than in the Anglesey Abbey version and moved the embarkation of the royal party into a more central position. Although Constable's difficulties are visible in a few areas where the surface paint has clearly been reworked more than once, the picture showed up particularly well among landscapes of similar date in the exhibition at the Tate.

After appearing at auction five times between 1838 and 1861, the picture was sold in 1891 by Agnew's to Sir Charles Tennant; his grandson, Lord Glenconner, sold it in 1955 through Leggatt's to Harry Ferguson; in 1987 it was sold anonymously through Agnew's to the Tate Gallery with assistance from the National Heritage Memorial Fund, the Clore Foundation, the National Art Collections Fund and many others.

The latest picture in date chosen for inclusion here is the extraordinary portrait by Richard Dadd, signed and dated 1852, of his physician, Sir Alexander Morison (1779-1866) (Plate 49).

Morison, an authority on mental diseases, had been appointed to a consultancy at Bethlem in 1835. It was he who helped Dadd to overcome the painter's 'block' which he had suffered on being committed to Bethlem for life in 1844 after he had murdered his father in August of the previous year.

The portrait was almost certainly commis-sioned by the sitter, whose house and estate at Anchorfield supply the background, while the boats on the river are a recollection of Dadd's boyhood at Chatham. The two fishwives, shown behind Morison, are based on his two daughters, one of whom, Anne, provided the sketch from which Dadd painted the landscape.

Dadd's intention, when a young man, 'to devote himself purely to works of imagination' is triumphantly fulfilled in this haunting portrait, where one hopes that Morison's somewhat distracted appearance is a reflection of the artist's mental state rather than of his own.

The picture was given to the Royal College of Physicians of Edinburgh by the sitter's grandson in 1927; in 1984 the College approached Agnew's with a view to selling it. It was sold by tender and the highest tender was submitted, most suitably, by the Scottish National Portrait Gallery.

The twenty pictures illustrated here do not represent all the acquisitions made from the firm by U.K. museums; purchases of Old Master drawings, sculpture, watercolours and modern pictures are recorded in the appropriate chapters of this volume. But one other picture deserves a mention: the delightful portrait by John Ellys (c.1701-1757) of *Mrs Hesta Booth*, the celebrated actress and dancer, in harlequin dress. This was sold at Sotheby's on 15 November 1989 (lot 34) and bought by Agnew's on behalf of the Victoria and Albert Museum for presentation to the Theatre Museum.

We should also like to record how pleased we were to be asked during the 1980s to value on behalf of the National Heritage Memorial Fund the contents of Kedleston, Weston Park and Belton. Dick Kingzett masterminded this mammoth undertaking by assembling a team of specialist valuers in various departments: furniture, silver, ceramics, textiles and so forth. And he did so again when we were asked by the V & A Museum in 1991 to carry out similar val-

Plate 18

JOHN CONSTABLE R.A.

1776-1837

The Opening of Waterloo Bridge

Oil on canvas, 53 x 86½ inches (135.7 x 220 cm.)

The Tate Gallery, London, 1987

uations at Ham House and Osterley Park.

In the last days of 1991, the Ipswich Borough Council managed to acquire a beautiful early landscape by Gainsborough of *Holywells Park, Ipswich* (Plate 19). Although much of the purchase price was contributed by the National Heritage Memorial Fund, the V & A Fund, the National Art Collections Fund and the Pilgrim Trust, the balance was raised locally by the Friends of the Ipswich Museums.

The picture, which has no known history before 1940 and has never been exhibited, was published by John Hayes in *The Landscape Paintings of Thomas Gainsborough* (1982) as '*Extensive Landscape with Reservoirs, Sluice Gate House and Seated Figure*'. Hayes dated the picture c. 1748-50 and drew attention to the strong influence of Jacob Ruisdael. He also mentioned a label on the back of the frame which was inscribed *The Nine Ponds at Hampstead*, but he demonstrated that the scene could not represent either Hamp-

stead or Highgate Ponds. Hayes did believe, however, that the view was probably not imaginary, and wrote, 'but no topographical expert has been able to suggest a credible source for it either in the London area or in East Anglia.' However, as soon as Norman Scarfe, the Suffolk archivist, saw a photograph, he identified the scene as Holywells Park, Ipswich, where there is just such a series of ponds, and other landmarks in the picture such as the windmill on the horizon and the two church spires were also shown to be topographically accurate.

The picture was therefore established as among the very small group of landscapes by Gainsborough which depict a recognisable view. Thus, in this case, correct identification of the scene has had the happy result of the picture going to the most appropriate place: Christchurch Mansion, Ipswich.

EVELYN JOLL

Plate 19

THOMAS GAINSBOROUGH R.A.

1727-88

Holywells Park, Ipswich

Oil on canvas, 20 x 26 inches (50.8 x 66 cm.)

Ipswich Borough Council Museums and Galleries, 1992

Chapter 2

MUSEUMS IN THE USA

GNEW'S CONNECTIONS WITH THE MAJOR museums of the USA have been close throughout the post-War period and many of the finest works of art we have handled have gone to them. During the decade of the 1980s, many of these museums have found their purchasing activities severely restricted by a combination of rising prices in the art market, rising administrative costs and static, or even falling, endowments and income. Even the tax laws (hitherto very favourable to donors of works of art to museums), were changed, though this may well turn out to be only a temporary aberration on the part of federal legislators. All these factors have meant that many US museums have passed through a difficult period, even though by the beginning of the '90s a more restrained market may have begun to tip the balance back again in their favour.

Of course the one exception to these generalisations has been the Getty Museum. Already well-endowed at the start of the decade, astute financial management of the Getty Trust has increased its endowment to an estimated \$3 billion today, and while part of its income goes to art-historical, educational and conservation projects, the major share is devoted to the museum's acquisition programmes. The use of such wealth and its implications for the art market has been much discussed both within the museum and outside. For some years there appeared to be some conflict between the immense power conferred by this wealth and the responsibilities implied by its proper use. As a result the museum was criticised for being able to buy whenever and wherever it might want and at the same time for being hesitant to

do so. In the boom market of the second half of the '80s, the Getty wealth became less conspicuous in comparison with the power of private collectors in the US and the influx of Japanese money into the market, and, as a consequence, it has perhaps been easier for the museum to pursue a more aggressive acquisition policy. When the new museum building opens its doors in some five years' time, its achievement will no doubt be judged primarily by the quality of its collections, and particularly by that of its European paintings. By then the addition of a further group of carefully selected masterpieces to an already eminent collection should mean that the expectations of its many visitors will not be disappointed.

In the early 1980s an eclectic range of acquisitions from Agnew's broadened the scope of the Getty's painting collection. Two very different van Dycks were purchased. The portrait of his first English patron, the Earl of Arundel (Plate 20), who was responsible for the introduction of the artist to the court of Charles I, is an extraordinarily sensitive characterisation of this fascinating patron of the arts. In contrast the sketch of *Saint Sebastian* (Plate 22), from the collection of Lord Clark, shows the other side of the artist's nature, as a painter of highly charged religious compositions. *The Virgin and Child with Saint John the Baptist* (Plate 23) by Guido Reni comes from the artist's last period, with its typical subdued colouring and poetic composition. No more beautiful example of Sebastiano Ricci's small-scale work could be found than the *Perseus and the head of Medusa* (Plate 28). Carlevaris is important as the first of the Venetian view painters, but his work is too often

Plate 20

SIR ANTHONY VAN DYCK

1599-1641

Thomas Howard, the Earl of Arundel

Oil on canvas, 40½ x 31¼ inches (102.8 x 79.4 cm.)

Collection of the J. Paul Getty Museum, Malibu, California, 1986

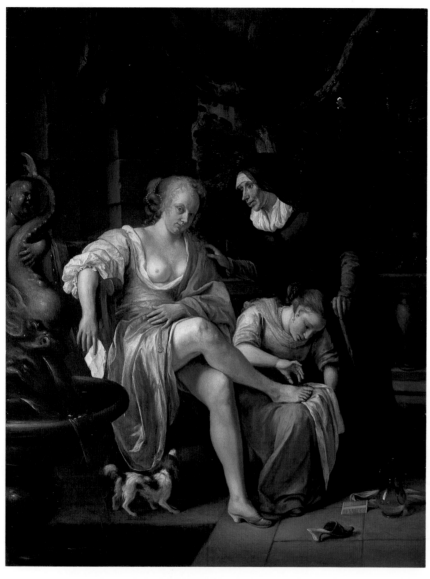

Plate 21 (above)

JAN STEEN

1625/6-1679

Bathsheba after the Bath

Oil on panel, 22⁷⁄₈ x 17³⁄₄ inches (58 x 45 cm.)

Collection of the J. Paul Getty Museum, Malibu, California, 1989

Plate 22 (below)

SIR ANTHONY VAN DYCK

1599-1641

St. Sebastian tended by an Angel

Oil on panel, 16 x 12 inches (40.5 x 30.5 cm.)

Collection of the J. Paul Getty Museum, Malibu, California, 1985

Plate 23

GUIDO RENI

1575-1642

The Virgin and Child with Saint John the Baptist

Oil on panel, 68 x 56 inches (172.7 x 142.3 cm.)

Collection of the J. Paul Getty Museum, Malibu, California, 1984

Plate 24 (above)

LUCA CARLEVARIS

1665-1731

A Regatta on the Grand Canal in Honour of Frederick IV,
King of Denmark

Oil on canvas, 53⅛ x 102¼ inches (134.9 x 259.7 cm.)

Collection of the J. Paul Getty Museum, Malibu, California, 1986

Plate 25 (below)

LUCA CARLEVARIS

1665-1731

The Bucintoro departing from
the Bacino di San Marco

Oil on canvas, 53¹/₁₆ x 102⅛ inches (134.7 x 259.3 cm.)

Collection of the J. Paul Getty Museum, Malibu, California, 1986

Plate 26

JACOPO CARUCCI CALLED PONTORMO

1494-1556

Portrait of a Halberdier

Oil (or oil and tempera) on panel transferred to canvas

36 ¼ x 28 ⅜ inches (92 x 72 cm.)

Collection of the J. Paul Getty Museum, Malibu, California, 1989

Plate 27

JOSEPH WRIGHT OF DERBY A.R.A.

1734-97

John Whetham of Kirklington

Oil on canvas, 50 x 40 inches (127 x 101.6 cm.)

Collection of the J. Paul Getty Museum, Malibu, California, 1985

Plate 28 (below)	Plate 29 (above)
SEBASTIANO RICCI	MEINDERT HOBBEMA
1659-1730	1638-1709
Perseus confronting Phineus with the Head of Medusa	*Wooded Landscape*
Oil on canvas, 25$\frac{3}{16}$ x 30$\frac{5}{16}$ inches (64 x 77 cm.)	Oil on wood, 24 x 33$\frac{1}{2}$ inches (61 x 81 cm.)
Collection of the J. Paul Getty Museum, Malibu, California, 1986	Collection of the J. Paul Getty Museum, Malibu, California, 1984

Plate 30

SEBASTIANO DEL PIOMBO

c.1485-1547

Pope Clement VII

Oil on slate, 41 ½ x 34 ½ inches (105.5 x 87.5 cm.)

Collection of the J. Paul Getty Museum, Malibu, California, 1991

repetitive and dull; no such criticism could be made of the Getty pair (Plates 24 and 25), once in the collection of a famous Italian film star, and extraordinary in their colour and vivacity. 17th century Dutch landscape is well illustrated by the small and charming Hobbema (Plate 29), and genre painting by Jan Steen's enticing *Bathsheba* (Plate 21). Lastly, in the field of English painting, John Whetham competes happily with his dog for the attention of the spectator in their portrait by Wright of Derby (Plate 27).

Important as these acquisitions were, they would have paled into insignificance beside the Nicolas Poussin of the *Finding of Moses* which Agnew's were able to offer to the Getty in 1986. Sadly the Getty refused our offer, but did buy the picture later from another dealer only to have the export licence refused and the Poussin purchased by the National Gallery. Perhaps had the original offer been accepted, the painting would now be in Malibu rather than in Trafalgar Square.

When in 1988 George Goldner, previously curator of drawings at the museum, added to his portfolio the curatorship of paintings, the direction of the acquisitions' policy of the Getty shifted significantly towards a concentration on the purchase of fewer paintings but of the highest quality. Since then Agnew's have been associated with the acquisition by the Getty of two major Old Master paintings. Pontormo's *Portrait of a Halberdier* (Plate 26) in 1989, was then and still is today at $35.2 million the most expensive Old Master painting ever sold. The picture had for many years been on loan to the Frick Collection in New York, and the decision by the owners to remove it from there and to sell one of the most important Old Masters still in private hands in the US created a considerable sense of shock in American museum circles. Discussion of a possible bid by the Getty for the painting began at an early stage between George

Goldner and myself, to the considerable benefit of the American telephone companies of whom he is a well-known patron. The final decision was only made after a visit to California and conversations with Harold Williams, the chief executive of the Getty Trust, and other trustees as well as the director and curator themselves - alternating with the summer delights of the swimming pool in the Bel Air hotel in Beverley Hills. Back in New York, the day of the auction provided, as usual, amusing incidents as well as the serious business of bidding for the picture. For security reasons it had been arranged that the limit of the museum's bid would only be made known to me by the deputy director of the museum when I was actually seated in the auction room. Unfortunately, I was unable to read the figure scribbled rather informally on a hand-written note as it was passed to me, and whispered confirmation of the amount into my ear was definitely a breach of hitherto well-maintained security. The actual bidding process was relatively simple (I have always felt it just as difficult to bid a small sum as a large one, and just as hair-raising) but I was delighted to secure the painting at a hammer price of $32 million in competition with an anonymous telephone bidder whose identity has never been revealed. The Getty not only added a major masterpiece of Florentine Mannerist portraiture to their collection, but also were seen to prevent the departure from American shores of what was being described almost in terms of a national treasure. Agnew's received world-wide publicity for their part in the purchase. While I was answering questions from the press at the back of the auction room, a collector in a neighbouring seat was seen to pick up our auction paddle and start to bid with it - though he just as rapidly put it down when it was pointed out to him that he might be held responsible for the payment for the Pontormo.

The other great masterpiece of Italian 16th

century portraiture acquired by the Getty is the Sebastiano del Piombo portrait of Pope Clement VII (Plate 30). The Pope, patron and friend of artists such as Raphael and Michelangelo, had fled from Rome after the Sack of 1527 which scattered the carefully cultivated artistic circle at the papal court. Alone of the artists from this circle, Sebastiano had stayed with him during his years of exile, and it was to him therefore that, after their return to the devastated Holy City in 1532, the task fell of painting an official portrait of the Pope. Clement is shown seated in a pose reminiscent of Raphael's *Julius II*, dressed in a richly painted red velvet tunic. His bearded face recalls his vow never to shave again in protest against the perpetrators of the Sack, his expression that of a man who has survived a traumatic shock but whose power is still formidable. Painted, unusually, on slate, this portrait reflects Sebastiano's mastery of technique and his extraordinary psychological insight into the character of his patron and friend.

The story of the picture in recent times is no less extraordinary than the portrait itself. Probably in the collection of the Earls of Pembroke at Wilton during the 19th century, it emerged only as 'Italian School - portrait of a Pope' in the catalogue of a Sotheby's sale in Chester in 1987. Bought by a dealer as a speculation for £170, the picture was taken to Christie's in London where, in spite of layers of dirt and discoloured varnish, it was quickly recognised by Sebastiano scholar Michael Hirst and put up for sale again. In partnership with New York's Newhouse Gallery we decided to bid for the painting and were immensely surprised to buy it against the reserve price for less than a quarter of our agreed limit. In a short time our enterprise was rewarded by its re-emergence fully revealed and in excellent condition, under the skilled hands of our restorer Sarah Walden. Now the picture has gone to join the Pontormo at the Getty as another pre-eminent example of

Italian 16th century portraiture.

The position of the Getty is of course exceptional amongst American museums but many of the other older established museums, even if less well endowed, have remained commendably active in their acquisitions. To the Metropolitan Museum went a Rubens landscape, one of the last in private hands, the mysterious nocturnal *Deer Hunt* (Plate 31), and to the Cloisters a rare early Nuremberg panel (Plate 32). Agnew's were able to contribute to the celebration in Washington of the 50th anniversary of the National Gallery with the purchase at auction of Ribera's *Martyrdom of St Bartholomew* (Plate 39), as well as the important and unusual Benjamin West *Expulsion of Adam and Eve* (Plate 38). To the Kimbell Museum in Fort Worth were added three contrasting pictures of exceptional interest - a rediscovered Mantegna *Holy Family* (Plate 34), a vibrant Rubens sketch (Plate 33) and the Domenichino *Abraham leading Isaac to Sacrifice* (Plate 45) from the Lansdowne collection. A yet more eclectic trio reflect the connoisseurship and taste of the director of the Cleveland Museum - a Heemskerk portrait, (Plate 41) a small Valdéz Leal on copper (Plate 44) and a magnificent landscape by the unjustly neglected Richard Wilson (Plate 40). A feeling for landscape paintings has been in fact a major feature of American museum buying over this period. Dallas imaginatively took the early Turner landscape of *Bonneville* (Plate 43), while the Museum of Fine Arts in Boston acquired one of Wright of Derby's finest Italian landscapes (Plate 42) in the year when the artist's importance was finally firmly established by an exemplary exhibition. The Huntington purchased its first Bonington, *View of Venice* (Plate 37), and continued its great tradition of collecting English portrait painting with the full-length portrait by van Dyck of *Mrs Kirke* (Plate 46), dresser to Queen Henrietta Maria, from the

Plate 31

Sir Peter Paul Rubens

1577-1640

A Forest at dawn with a Deer Hunt

Oil, with traces of black chalk underdrawing, on panel

24 x 35 inches (62 x 90 cm.)

The Metropolitan Museum of Art, 1990 (In association with the Artemis Group)

collection at Parham Park. The Yale Center for British Art acquired a small pre-Raphaelite portrait by Ford Madox Brown, *The Irish Girl* (Plate 36), and Paul Mellon most generously gave them the beautiful Bonington *Beached Vessels and a Wagon near Trouville* (Plate 35) which he had bought in 1986 from my father (his last sale to his best client shortly before his death). Such an interesting diversity of museum acquisitions shows that there is still a great reserve of vitality in these institutions which has survived even in difficult circumstances.

JULIAN AGNEW

Plate 33 (below)

Sir Peter Paul Rubens

1577-1640

The Martyrdom of St. Ursula and the 11,000 Maidens

Oil sketch on panel, 25³⁄₈ x 19³⁄₈ inches (64.4 x 49.3 cm.)

The Kimbell Art Museum, Fort Worth, Texas, 1985

(In association with E V Thaw and Co. Inc.)

Plate 32 (above)

Unknown German (Nuremberg) Painter 14th century

The Bishop of Assisi handing a palm to Saint Clare

Tempera and gold on oak panel 13¼ x 8⅝ inches (33.5 x 22 cm.)

The Metropolitan Museum of Art, New York, The Cloisters

Collection, 1984 (1984.343)

Plate 34

ANDREA MANTEGNA

1431-1506

Holy Family with St. Elizabeth and the Infant St. John the Baptist

Distemper and gold on canvas, 24³/₄ x 20 ¹/₄ inches (62.9 x 51.3 cm.)

The Kimbell Art Museum, Fort Worth, Texas, 1986

(In association with the Newhouse Gallery)

Plate 35

RICHARD PARKES BONINGTON

1802-28

Beached Vessels and a Wagon near Trouville

Oil on canvas, 14 ¾ x 20 ⅝ inches (37.1 x 52.2 cm.)

Yale Center for British Art, Paul Mellon Collection, 1986 (B1986.29.1)

Plate 36 (above)

FORD MADOX BROWN

1821-93

The Irish Girl

Oil on canvas laid on board, 11¼ x 10 inches (28.5 x 27.3 cm.)

Yale Center for British Art, Paul Mellon Fund, 1989 (B1989.11)

Plate 37 (below)

RICHARD PARKES BONINGTON

1802-28

View of Venice

Oil on board, 12 x 16 inches (30.5 x 40.6 cm.)

Henry E. Huntington Library and Art Gallery, 1983

Plate 38

BENJAMIN WEST P.R.A.

1738-1820

The Expulsion of Adam and Eve from Paradise

Oil on canvas, 73⁹⁄₁₆ x 109½ inches (1.868 x 2.781 m.)

National Gallery of Art, Washington; Avalon Fund and Patrons'

Permanent Fund, 1989

Plate 39

JUSEPE RIBERA

1591-1652

Martyrdom of St. Bartholomew

Oil on canvas, 41 x 44 inches (104 x 113 cm.)

National Gallery of Art, 1991. Washington, Gift of the 50th

Anniversary Gift Committee.

Plate 40

RICHARD WILSON R.A.

1713/14 - 82

The Valley of the Mawddach with Cader Idris Beyond

Oil on Canvas, 35³/₈ x 41¹/₄ inches (89.8 x 105.5 cm.)

The Cleveland Museum of Art, 1987 (87.7). Leonard C. Hanna, Jnr., Fund.

Plate 41

MAERTEN VAN HEEMSKERK

1498-1574

Machtelt Suijs, Wife of Dirick van Teijlingen

Oil on panel, 33 ½ x 29 ⅛ inches (85 x 74 cm.)

The Cleveland Museum of Art, 1987 (87.136). Leonard C. Hanna, Jnr., Fund.

Plate 42

JOSEPH WRIGHT OF DERBY A.R.A.

1734-97

A Grotto in the Kingdom of Naples with Banditti

Oil on canvas, 48 x 68 inches (122 x 175 cm.)

Museum of Fine Arts, Boston, 1990. Charles H. Bayley

Picture and Painting Fund and other Funds, by exchange.

Plate 43

J.M.W. TURNER R.A.

1775-1851

Bonneville, Savoy with Mont Blanc

Oil on canvas, 36¼ x 48½ inches (91.5 x 122 cm.)

Dallas Museum of Art, Foundation for the Arts Collection, 1985

Plate 44 (above)

JUAN DE VALDÉS LEAL

1622-90

The Assumption of the Virgin

Oil on panel, 15 ½ x 10 inches (39.5 x 25.5 cm.)

The Cleveland Museum of Art, 1987 (87.136).

Leonard C. Hanna, Jnr., Fund.

Plate 45 (below)

DOMENICO ZAMPIERI CALLED DOMENICHINO

1581-1641

Abraham leading Isaac to Sacrifice

Oil on copper, 12 ½ x 17 ½ inches (32.5 x 44.3 cm.)

The Kimbell Art Museum, Fort Worth,

Texas, 1982

Plate 46

SIR ANTHONY VAN DYCK

1599-1641

Mrs Kirke

Oil on canvas, 87¾ x 51½ inches (207 x 130.8 cm.)

Henry E. Huntington Library and Art Gallery, 1983

[55]

Chapter 3

'IDEAS FROM HEAVEN'

JOHN SINGLETON COPLEY WAS UNDOUBT-
edly the most accomplished of American
18th century portrait painters and the only
one to achieve an international reputation.
In 1984 Agnew's handled first one, then a
second of his greatest women's portraits
through a successful venture into what was, for
us, a hitherto uncharted area of the art market.

The sitter in the first portrait was Mrs
Thomas Gage (Plate 47), the daughter of Captain Stephen Kemble of New York and the wife
of General Sir Thomas Gage. Her husband,
commander-in-chief of the British forces in
America from 1763 to 1772 and Governor of
Massachusetts from 1774 to 1775, was responsible for a series of tactless measures aimed at
subduing the restless colonists, and succeeded in
provoking an incident at Lexington in 1775
which may be said to have sparked off the War
of Independence; following the inconclusive
battle at Bunker's Hill he resigned amid univer-
sal criticism. His portrait had been painted by
Copley in 1768/9, a picture purchased at auction in New York in 1971 by Agnew's on behalf
of Mr Paul Mellon and now in the Yale Center
for British Art. This portrait was instrumental
in establishing the reputation of the largely self-
taught artist outside his native town of Boston,
and in the summer of 1771 Copley came to
New York to carry out a series of portrait commissions organised by Stephen Kemble, of
which the most important was that of Kemble's
daughter Mrs Gage.

The sitter is shown in an elaborate and
unusual contrapostal pose, her head supported
on her hand and with a faraway gaze in her
eyes; one London critic wrote of her that after
'having stared into her plain face and dreaming
eyes for three quarters of an hour' he was still
unable to decide whether she was about to
laugh or to cry. Echoes of 17th century Italian
painting, particularly of Domenichino, no doubt
the result of the artist's correspondence with
Reynolds in England, and hints of the neo-classical movement to come, combine with the lus-
cious paint texture of Mrs Gage's dress and of
the sofa to create an unforgettable image, all
suffused with the direct, hard and clear vision of
the New World. Sent over to London for exhibition in 1772, to test the water for a possible
move across the Atlantic by the artist himself, it
not surprisingly received a rapturous reception.
Copley himself, who did in fact settle in England in 1774, had no doubt of its quality. In
1771 he wrote to Henry Pelham, 'I have done
some of my best portraits here, particularly Mrs
Gage's, which has gone to the Exhibition. It is I
think beyond Compare the best Lady's portrait
I ever Drew; but Mr Pratt says of it, It will be
flesh and Blood these 200 years to come, that
every Part and line in it is Butifull [*sic.*], that I
must get my Ideas from Heaven.'

From the time of the London exhibition the
painting remained at Firle Place in Sussex, the
Gage family home, and the identities of both
artist and sitter were in the course of time for-
gotten, until in 1938 they were correctly re-
established. Following the death of the sixth
Viscount Gage in 1983, the family decided to
sell the painting in order to set up a mainte-
nance fund for the house and turned to Agnew's
with whom there had been (and remains) a long
and happy connection, to carry out the sale.
The situation was an unusual one and demanded

Plate 47

JOHN SINGLETON COPLEY R.A.

1738-1815

Mrs Thomas Gage

Oil on canvas, 50 x 40 inches (127 x 116 cm.)

The Putnam Foundation, The Timken Museum of Art, San Diego, 1984

Plate 48

JOHN SINGLETON COPLEY R.A.

1738-1815

Portrait of a Woman, probably Miss Johnston

Oil on canvas, 48½ x 39½ inches (123.2 x 100.4 cm.)

Los Angeles County Museum of Art, Museum Acquisition Fund

1985 (85.2)

an unusual solution. Both before and repeatedly after Lord Gage's death, the family and Agnew's had been approached by buyers from the USA interested in this major masterpiece of early American painting. On the other hand the record of Copley prices both at auction and privately was very patchy. In the circumstances we concluded that the best method to sell the painting was by sealed-bid tender; this enabled the various potential buyers to set the price in competition with each other, yet left control of the process firmly in the hands of the owners. It was arranged to exhibit the picture in New York and London prior to the tender date; publicity for the tender was carefully planned, with a suggested price of over $1 million (the auction record for a Copley still being the $210,000 paid for the portrait of General Gage 13 years earlier).

The New York exhibition of Mrs Gage was arranged at the National Academy of Design, a highly suitable and attractive venue for its display, and attracted considerable coverage in the press. Two beautiful console tables, contemporary with the painting, were borrowed from a New York private collector and displayed on either side of the painting. Each day began with the ritual removal of two vases of flowers which threatened to damage their polished surfaces; nevertheless the vases would mysteriously reappear yet again the following morning. The opening party was a rather subdued event because of a two-foot fall of snow in the city that evening, so only the intrepid few managed to get to it. Among them was David Bull, formerly a commercial picture restorer in London, subsequently director of the Norton Simon Museum in California and now chairman of the conservation department of the National Gallery in Washington. Over the next 10 days we managed to bring in front of the picture most of the major collectors, museum directors and dealers interested in American paintings, and it was

clear that great excitement over the painting was being generated. Curiosity over the method of sale, mixed with a degree of envy, dominated the New York trade; a group of dealers entertained me to lunch and grilled me over the details of the sale almost as comprehensively as the fish that was served as a main course. Amongst those most obviously impressed by the painting was a mid-West collector, himself also a member of a powerful and prestigious committee devoted to furthering the decoration of the White House. By the end of the New York showing we were confident of achieving an excellent result for the tender.

Back in London, however, the impetus seemed to fade over the remaining days before the closing date. One sealed envelope arrived from a New York dealer, but no further word was heard from the mid-West collector. A few hours before closing time in London on the evening preceding the noon deadline for tenders, I telephoned the director of the Los Angeles County Museum, who had expressed interest in the painting during the New York showing. Indeed he was interested, the museum was going to make a bid, but surely there were another five days before the tender closed? A series of frantic calls ensued over the rest of the evening and lasted way into the night, punctuated on my side by the demands of an ill and querulous 18-month-old baby. By the morning a definite bid had been put together and confirmed, and at noon we met to open the sealed envelopes; the New York dealer's was the higher of the two and was accepted.

Gradually over the next few weeks the full story began to emerge. David Bull, who had fought his way to the opening party in New York, had recommended the picture to the Timken Museum of Art in San Diego, to whom he was an unofficial adviser. Unable to find the cash to buy the picture outright, the museum had made an arrangement with the New York dealer that he should tender for the Copley and if successful should take a painting by Frederick Remington, an artist well-known for his scenes of cowboy life, in exchange. The White House committee had indeed been most enthusiastic about buying the picture and had even secured the funds for a pre-emptive bid when their plans were suddenly vetoed at a level next only to that of the President himself. Nor did the successful conclusion of the tendering process bring the story to an end. An export licence was required for the picture and our application was referred to the Reviewing Committee by Michael Levey, the director of the National Gallery in London, on the grounds that the painting was of outstanding aesthetic importance. Against that we could not argue, but nevertheless the committee decided not to delay the export, being most visibly swayed by a casual remark of one of its members that 'it was certainly not a million pound picture' - a rather strange conclusion in that amid a sea of subjective opinions, the price realised was the one objective fact. After the meeting, a rather dejected Michael Levey confided in us that while he had not had the funds available some six months before when we had first told him of the impending sale, he now did so and would definitely have bought the painting, had the licence been delayed! So after a series of vagaries which could easily have meant a final home in either Los Angeles, Washington or London, Mrs Gage came to rest in San Diego, where, expertly cleaned by David Bull, she hangs in her full glory today.

From Agnew's point of view, the story of *Mrs Gage* had two direct results. First, the process of the tender had been successful enough to justify a further sale by this method, that of Richard Dadd's *Sir Alexander Morison* (Plate 49). Nevertheless the tender process was generally held by most potential buyers to be too favourable to the seller to be a successful marketing device except on the rarest occasions. Secondly the sale led directly to the appearance on the market of a second woman's portrait by Copley (Plate 48), also one of the New York commissions and arguably as high in quality as *Mrs Gage* herself. This painting had also come from an old English collection, was also wrongly attributed to Nathaniel Dance and had only recently been correctly identified. The sitter, probably a Miss Johnston, is shown seated on the same sofa, presumably a studio prop, as Mrs Gage, though it is here covered in red rather than blue. The letter she holds is dated 1771, establishing the portrait as part of the New York series. The pose of the sitter, the richness of the materials and the strong *chiaroscuro*, invites comparison between the two paintings, but Miss Johnston's direct gaze towards the spectator differentiates the mood from Mrs Gage's faraway and contemplative look.

The second time around, the process of selling a Copley was less complicated. The obvious buyer was the Los Angeles County Museum, and after a long and hard-fought round of bargaining, a price satisfactory to both buyer and seller was agreed upon. This time there was no export problem as the picture had been for many years in the USA, Miss Johnston was able freely to join Mrs Gage in California, and two of Copley's most beautiful 'ideas from heaven' had found new homes on earth.

JULIAN AGNEW

Plate 49

RICHARD DADD

1817-86

Sir Alexander Morison

Oil on canvas, 19⁷/₈ x 24 inches (55 x 60.9 cm.)

The Scottish National Portrait Gallery, 1984

Chapter 4

GOYA'S MARQUESA DI SANTA CRUZ

OR A FIRST-CLASS GOYA PORTRAIT TO appear on the art market is always a rare event, and it was therefore a matter for considerable excitement when, in early 1986, Christie's announced they were going to auction the *Marquesa di Santa Cruz* (Plate 50). The picture itself had always been a celebrated one, generally acknowledged as one of the artist's finest creations - indeed a masterpiece. The sitter was the daughter of one of Goya's most influential early patrons, the Duke of Osuna, and as a child of four she appears with her parents and brothers and sisters in the famous family portrait now in the Prado. In 1801 she married the heir to the Santa Cruz titles and three years later Lady Holland, who met her in the course of a visit to Spain, wrote the following description: 'very beautiful; a most engaging, captivating smile when she speaks'. In this portrait of 1805, she is shown lying full-length on a *lit-de-repos*, her head wreathed with grapes and vine-leaves and holding a lyre-guitar. It is perhaps the most obviously neo-classical of all Goya's portraits and even though at the time the quality of the handling was much obscured by layers of dirt and discoloured varnish, the extraordinary contrast of the Marquesa's white dress, the deep red of the day bed and the dark background was clearly visible. (Since the painting entered the Prado, the painting has been carefully and sensitively cleaned, revealing the full glory of its many subtleties). The painting had remained in the family hands until 1947,

having achieved a certain notoriety in the War period when General Franco is said to have considered purchasing it to give as a wedding present to his fellow-dictator Hitler, no doubt attracted to it by the general resemblance to a swastika of the sound hole on the musical instrument.

The appearance of such an important Goya outside Spain was in itself a matter for public comment, but the circumstance of its proposed sale became even more surprising in the light of a special condition in the Christie's catalogue: '...the seller is selling only such title as it has to the picture... Purchasers should take their own advice. Further information as to the recent history of the picture is available from the seller'. Such a condition of sale was, to say the least, unusual, and probably unprecedented in the history of the salerooms in modern times, but gradually its purpose became clear as the recent history of the picture unfolded.

Until 1983, the painting had remained in Spain, first in the hands of the collector who had purchased it in 1947 and subsequently of his widow, from whom it had been bought by a Mr Saorin Bosch. In that year it was exported to Zurich where it was purchased by companies ultimately owned by trustees of the Wimborne family trusts on whose behalf Christie's were offering the picture. Of course for a picture of this importance to leave the country, an export licence would be required from the Spanish authorities and Mr Bosch was able to produce

Plate 50

<small>FRANCISCO JOSÉ DE GOYA Y LUCIENTES</small>

1746-1828

Marquesa di Santa Cruz

Oil on canvas, 49 ¼ x 81 ¾ inches (125.2 x 207.8 cm.)

Museo del Prado, Madrid, 1986

documents to satisfy the prospective purchasers that the export of the painting had been properly and legally sanctioned.

Within a short time the picture had been offered by the new owners to the Getty Museum at a price of $12 million. In the course of their consideration of the picture, the museum consulted an American expert on Goya, who in turn, surprised by the presence of the painting outside Spain, consulted colleagues in the Prado. They were more than surprised that the picture had left the country, and immediately questioned the legal validity of its export. In July 1983, the Spanish government

informed the Getty that the picture had been removed from Spain without an export licence and the museum ceased to consider its purchase.

The essence of the problem which was to surround the picture until its resolution some three years later was now clear. The Wimborne family trusts in buying the painting had believed that its export from Spain had been legally sanctioned; they had therefore good legal title to it. If however, as the Spanish government now claimed, the export documents were forgeries, and the export therefore illegal, no reputable buyer anywhere in the world was going to purchase the painting. Negotiations were opened between the owners and the Spanish authorities to try to resolve this stalemate, but dragged on unsuccessfully until late in 1985 when the owners delivered an ultimatum that, unless a solution had been found by 17 January in the new year, the announcement would be made of the proposed sale of the picture at auction.

It was at this stage that Agnew's first became involved in this difficult and delicate situation. As chairman of an inter-trade committee, I had recently been involved in the drawing up of a code of conduct, which had been generally adopted by both auctioneers and dealers, to prevent trading in works of art which had been stolen or illegally exported from their country of origin. While there was obviously no question of the former, it did appear that if the Goya had been illegally exported from Spain, Christie's would be in breach of the code if they tried to sell it. One of the advisers to the Wimborne family, and an old friend, wary of the possible adverse consequences for the sale of the painting if the code was invoked, started to consult me on the one hand, while on the other Matthew Farrer, senior partner of Agnew's own solicitors, approached me for advice on behalf of the Spanish government, by whom he had been instructed. A case was in fact soon before the courts by which the Spanish government sought to obtain a declaration that the purported export documents were forgeries and that, if so, the export of the picture from Spain was illegal. Yet, even though a preliminary judgement went in the Spaniards' favour, there was no time before the proposed sale date for the courts to hear the case on the substantial issue, and in any case the Spanish government had no claim to legal ownership of the painting. For some weeks, I hovered uneasily between all the parties, attempting to give disinterested advice to both sides and to convince Christie's of their obligations under the code of conduct.

It became increasingly clear to me that the only way to cut through the intricate legal and commercial situation was for the Spanish government to purchase the picture from the Wimborne family trusts and to bring it back to Spain, thus solving the problems of both ownership and of illegal export at the same time. But how was it possible for Agnew's to act without any standing in this case? In a typically unconventional solution, Lord Wimborne's adviser suggested that I should become an official adviser to the Spanish government, a proposal that Matthew Farrer graciously accepted. (This must indeed be one of the few cases where a client has suggested that Agnew's should act for the opposite party in a dispute!) The pressure was now on to resolve the matter as quickly as possible. The sale was only a week away, and a few days later there was to be the first visit to Britain of the Spanish royal family since Franco's death, an event which clearly the British government did not wish to see marred by a dispute over the Goya. Matthew Farrer and I set off for Madrid, and spent the day kicking our heels in the waiting-room of the relevant minister while various attempts were made to invoke help from other parties. Eventually, with only half an hour available before we had to leave to catch our flight back to London, we were admitted, but during that time we were able to convince the minister that we had to have a definite offer figure to which the Spanish government were prepared to go for the picture and within which we were authorised to negotiate. The principle was established, the flight caught (just), and the figure confirmed by a late night telephone call to London. Breakfast the next morning with the Wimborne advisers in a London hotel produced a figure from their side, and within a few hours, with the able assistance of Jo Floyd, then chairman of Christie's, who had taken personal charge of the negotiations, the principles of a satisfactory agreement had been condensed by Matthew Farrer into a single typewritten page. We had however not reckoned with the solicitors for the Wimborne trusts who appeared with a myriad of black briefcases and settled down to 'boiler-plate' the agreement into exhaustive legal form. Negotiations continued until the early hours of the morning and several times looked as if they might break down over the legal position of the dealer who had acted as an intermediary for the owner in the purchase of the painting; a warrant for his arrest had been issued by the Spanish legal authorities. At one point Lord Wimborne himself, who had joined his team, walked out of the meeting, but whether through anger or boredom was not clear. Finally, following a further exhaustive and exhausting all-day meeting an agreement, now the size of a small book, was signed by all parties and an even more complex negotiation over a public announcement of the withdrawal of the picture from the auction concluded.

The basis of the agreement was that the Goya became, in the delicate phrasing of the press release, 'the property of the Spanish state' in return for a payment of $6 million. This figure was intended to represent not only a fair compensation to the owners for their investment in the picture but also the price which the painting might have fetched on the Spanish internal market without the benefit of foreign competition. Agnew's were particularly well-placed to advise on this aspect of the price level, since we had recently bought at auction in Spain the small Goya, *Flight of the Witches* (Plate 53) which was also an 'unexportable picture', and this proved most useful as a comparative base. Though neither party was totally happy as to the eventual figure, the pressure of the situation was such that eventually both agreed to what was indeed a fair price.

Within a few days of agreement being reached, the diminutive Manuela Mena from the Prado Museum appeared in London to take charge of the painting, revealing a striking resemblance in her personal appearance to the Marquesa herself. It was rather nervously that I accompanied her down to Christie's to inspect the painting; if she were to pronounce it a copy by Esteve, how were we to unravel all the negotiations of the previous ten days? Even more nervously we awaited the arrival of an official from the Spanish Finance Ministry, who was carrying the cheque for the purchase price, but who had disappeared in London during the previous 24 hours. Luckily Manuela was delighted with the picture, the official appeared on time only slightly the worse for wear, and the Goya was taken off to Agnew's for a celebratory press conference and party. The next morning the painting was carried off to the airport in a convoy of wailing police sirens and thence to its eventual final destination in the Prado.

In retrospect, the negotiated solution of the complex problems surrounding the Goya 'Marquesa' was a happy one for all the parties concerned. The owners were pleased to be free from the problems of holding or selling the painting and to receive adequate and reasonable compensation for it. The Prado acquired a magnificent Goya, one of the finest in private hands and a major addition to their extraordinary representation of the artist. The London art trade were seen to behave responsibly and ethically in a difficult situation and Agnew's were delighted to have played a part in the satisfactory resolution of the problems surrounding the sale of the picture. Yet one or two questions still remain to be answered. How was the picture originally exported from Spain before its arrival in Zurich? By plane to Buenos Aires via an overnight boat to Majorca? How and by whom were the forged documents produced? Perhaps in time the final details of the strange and fascinating story of this beautiful picture will be revealed.

JULIAN AGNEW

Chapter 5

THE ORTIZ-PATIÑO COLLECTION

THE COLLECTION OF PAINTINGS AND DRAW-INGS formed by Jaime Ortiz-Patiño through Agnew's is probably one of the most distinguished private collections with which the firm has ever been associated. Grandson of the Bolivian 'King of Tin' Simon Patiño, Jaime Ortiz-Patiño has the family passion for collecting, extending not only through the range of Old Master and Impressionist paintings and drawings, but also of silver, gold boxes, books and furniture. Many of his collections he has dispersed, some within a few years of their formation, but usually only with the intention of forming yet another. For some the 'disease' of collecting has only an acute phase; for others such as Jaime Ortiz-Patiño it is chronic.

To begin with, the emphasis was on Francesco Guardi. It was a surprise to me when one day in 1982 I was telephoned by a hitherto unknown caller who asked me to report on a pair of Guardi capricci which were coming up at auction. Pausing only to confirm with a dealer friend that I was not the victim of an elaborate hoax, I went off to inspect the paintings and reported back favourably. A limit for the bid was agreed, and the pictures bought well within the limit. A few weeks later we met for the first time in front of the paintings, the first of a series of meetings in London, New York, Geneva, Madrid and Sotogrande where fine paintings have been discussed, good food consumed and pleasant conversations enjoyed.

Two Guardi *vedute* were soon added to this first purchase; the silvery *San Giorgio Maggiore* (Plate 51), one of a pair formerly divided between the two Californian collectors Edward Carter and Norton Simon, and the shimmering *Rio dei Mendicanti* (Plate 52). In addition a pair of fine capricci were at one time in the collection, together with a small Canaletto *Torre di Malghera*; now all three are reunited under one roof in the United States (see Plates 71, 72 and 73). The horizons of the collection began to widen with the addition of the Goya *Flight of the Witches* (Plate 53) in 1985, one of a series of six paintings on witchcraft painted for the Duchess of Osuna, other examples of the series being now in the London National Gallery and Museo Lazaro Galdiano in Madrid. A small group of Spanish paintings was soon joined by Murillo's *Virgin and Child* (Plate 54), a preparatory sketch for a large oil in the Prado.

Then the emphasis changed towards the Northern Schools. The van Dyck portrait of the *Earl of Arundel* (Plate 20) passed through the collection and subsequently on to the Getty Museum. The superb Rubens sketch shows the Virgin and Child venerated by eight saints (Plate 55), among them St. Elizabeth of Hungary, the patron of the Archduchess Isabella Clara Eugenia who may have commissioned an altarpiece for which this sketch was preparatory but which was never completed. Uytewael is an artist whose reputation has increased by leaps and bounds over the last decade, the Ortiz-Patiño example (Plate 57) is arguably the finest of the

Plate 51 (above)

FRANCESCO GUARDI

1712-93

San Giorgio Maggiore, Venice

Oil on canvas, 16 x 19³/₄ inches (40.6 x 50.2 cm.)

Collection of Jaime Ortiz-Patiño, 1985

Plate 52 (below)

FRANCESCO GUARDI

1712-93

Rio dei Mendicanti

Oil on canvas, 20 x 30 inches (51 x 76 cm.)

Collection of Jaime Ortiz-Patiño, 1985

Plate 53

FRANCISCO JOSÉ DE GOYA Y LUCIENTES

1746-1828

The Flight of the Witches (Vuelo de Brujas)

Oil on canvas, 17 ⅛ x 12 inches (43.5 x 30.5 cm.)

Collection of Jaime Ortiz-Patiño, 1985

Plate 54

Bartolome Esteban Murillo

1617-1682

Virgin and Child

Oil on panel, 11 x 7¾ inches (28 x 20 cm.)

Collection of Jaime Ortiz-Patiño, 1988

Plate 55

SIR PETER PAUL RUBENS

1577-1640

Virgin and Child with eight Saints

Oil on panel, 13¼ x 20½ inches (35 x 53 cm.)

Collection of Jaime Ortiz-Patiño, 1987

Plate 56

EGLON HENDRICK VAN DER NEER

1634?-1703

Figures in an Interior

Oil on canvas, 33 ¾ x 27 ½ inches (85.7 x 69.9 cm.)

Collection of Jaime Ortiz-Patiño, 1987

Plate 57

JOACHIM UYTEWAEL (OR WTEWAEL)

1566-1638

The Golden Age

Oil on copper, 8⅞ x 11⅞ inches (22.5 x 30.2 cm.)

Collection of Jaime Ortiz-Patiño, 1988

Plate 58

PHILIPS WOUVERMANS

1619-68

Stag Hunt

Oil on copper, 11 x 14 inches (27 x 35 cm.)

Collection of Jaime Ortiz-Patiño, 1989

Plate 59

HENRI FANTIN-LATOUR

1836-1904

Asters et Fruits sur une Table

Oil on canvas, 22½ x 29½ inches (56.5 x 55 cm.)

Collection of Jaime Ortiz-Patiño, 1986

Plate 60

PIERRE-AUGUSTE RENOIR

1841-1919

Couple Lisant

Oil on canvas 12 ¾ x 9 ¾ inches (56 x 46 cm.)

Collection of Jaime Ortiz-Patiño, 1983

small coppers which have appeared on the market over the period. The Wouvermans (Plate 58), unusually for him is also painted on copper, which gives it a beautiful luminosity, while the Eglon van der Neer (Plate 56) is a fine example of a sophisticated interior by this rare painter.

The formation of an exceptional group of Impressionist paintings started in 1983 with the acquisition at auction of the small Renoir, *Couple Lisant* (Plate 60), formerly in the McCormick, Norton Simon and Henry Ford II collections. A year later the purchase of the Gauguin *Mata Mua* (Plate 61) was a major coup. It was arranged that the purchase of this painting should be jointly shared with Baron Thyssen; whilst I bid in person in the room, the latter on the telephone from Japan resolutely refused to participate in the bidding to the evident consternation of the auctioneers. (Five years later the painting, which had been bought for $3.82 million, was resold at auction for just over $24 million, Baron Thyssen eventually taking over ownership of the whole.)

In the years following the Gauguin purchase, I was able to arrange (with the co-operation of Desmond Corcoran of the Lefevre Gallery and of Eugene Thaw in New York) for three masterpieces to enter the Ortiz-Patiño collection. The Cézanne *Still-life* (Plate 62), once in the Barnes, Chester Beatty and Rockefeller collections, is on the surface a miracle of lucid and radiant colour, but hiding within it is a complex pattern of extraordinary spatial relationships. The Fantin-Latour (Plate 59) is also a majestic formal still-life but enlivened by the glittering

brush strokes and textures of his artistry. (It has now entered the Metropolitan Museum as part of the Annenberg collection). Above all the Monet of *Zaandam* (Plate 63) encapsulates for me the fresh and vivid charm of the best decade of French Impressionism. To see this painting, bought just a few days before my father's death, auctioned in 1989 with the rest of the carefully chosen group of Impressionist pictures was for me a moment of particular sadness.

If the heart of the collection has always been in paintings, the few, but select, Old Master drawings should not be ignored. Among the French drawings there is one of the finest pages from the Odescalchi album of Claude drawings, a large scale sketch from life of the notary for Greuze's celebrated *L'Accordée de Village* (see Plate 131), and the brilliant and sensitive Chassériau portrait drawing of *Raymond de Magnancourt* (see Plate 130). Italy in the 18th century is represented by one of the finest Tiepolo drawings from the Orloff album (see Plate 132), and the mysterious and evocative Guardi *Fishing Boats* (see page 133) from the collection of John Nicholas Brown.

At the time of writing it has just been announced that further sales from the collection are about to take place. It is the privilege of a collector to buy and sell as he wishes; it is the privilege of a dealer to consider that a work of art he has once handled is in a sense forever his. Maybe in the future the ebb and flow of the art market will carry other pictures from Agnew's to the Ortiz-Patiño collection.

JULIAN AGNEW

Plate 61

PAUL GAUGUIN

1848-1903

Mata Mua — in olden times

Oil on canvas, 37 x 28 inches (93 x 72 cm.)

Collection of Jaime Ortiz-Patiño, 1984

Plate 62

PAUL CÉZANNE

1839-1906

Nature Morte à la Draperie Bleu

Oil on paper mounted on panel, 16½ x 28⅜ inches (42 x 72 cm.)

Collection of Jaime Ortiz-Patiño, 1986

Plate 63

CLAUDE MONET

1840-1926

The Garden House on the Banks of the Zaan, Zaandam

Oil on canvas, 21 ½ x 29 inches (54 x 74 cm.)

Collection of Jaime Ortiz-Patiño, 1984

Chapter 6

COLLECTORS WORLDWIDE

Plate 64

AMICO ASPERTINI

1474-1552

A Cleric Holding a Scroll

Oil on panel, 24½ x 19¼ inches (62.5 x 48.5 cm.)

Private collection, 1990

Vasari described Aspertini as 'an eccentric man of extravagant brain, whose figures executed by him throughout all of Italy are equally eccentric and even mad, if one may say so'.

Aspertini was trained in Ferrara under Ercole Roberti, then went to Rome from 1500-1503, before returning to his native town, Bologna, where he painted this portrait, in about 1515. During his time in Rome he must have seen wall paintings which surely influenced the extraordinary landscape background here.

The picture belonged to George Salting, a major client of Agnew's, who liked to conclude deals with the firm on an island in the middle of Piccadilly. When Salting died in 1910, he left most of his collection of pictures to the National Gallery; but the Aspertini passed to his niece, who married the Earl of Haddington from whose collection Agnew's bought it in 1987.

EJ

Plate 65

GENTILE DA FABRIANO

c.1370-1427

The Annunciation

Oil on panel, 16⅛ x 19¼ inches (41 x 49 cm.)

Mrs Seward Johnson, 1986 (In association with the Matthiesen Gallery)

Keith Christiansen dates this picture 1419-20. When his monograph on Gentile was published in 1982 the composition was known only in a work of poor quality in the Vatican by an unknown follower of Gentile. In 1986 our picture appeared in a sale in Paris and was immediately recognised as the original. It was reputedly bought in Florence in 1860 by the Countess Ducros and then descended in her family.

Christiansen suggests that this was probably painted at the beginning of Gentile's time in Florence, not as a specific commission but intended for general sale. The *predella* panels of *The Adoration of the Magi*, painted for the Strozzi Chapel in Santa Trinità but now in the Uffizi, have close parallels to this picture.

While the graceful innocence of the two figures seems characteristic of pre-Renaissance painting, Gentile's skill in depicting light and recession in the composition, as well as the sense of form in some of the objects in the room anticipate the work of Masaccio.

EJ

Plate 66

GIOVANNI ANTONIO PELLEGRINI

1675-1741

Bacchus and Ariadne

Oil on canvas, 15 x 43 inches (38 x 109 cm.)

Private collection, Canada, 1985

This enchanting over-door is an example of a Venetian painter working in this country for a grand English house, in this instance that belonging to the Fountaine family, in Norfolk. Pellegrini was actually brought to England by the Earl of Manchester in 1708 and at this time Sir Andrew Fountaine, a distinguished connoisseur and collector, commissioned Pellegrini to undertake a decorative scheme for his house, Narford Hall.

Bacchus and Ariadne is not connected with any of the main decoration at Narford and is an additional work painted at the time of the original commission. This picture is instead more closely related to a larger bacchanal formerly in the Paul Wallraf Collection and exhibited at the Royal Academy in 1960 (*Italian Art in Britain* no. 451) and a drawing of the same subject sold at Christie's (July 4, 1978, lot 63).

Pellegrini is usually cited as one of the foremost pioneers of Rococo Venetian painting and his presence in England in the early 18th century influenced the development of the Rococo movement in English decoration.

RM

Plate 67

GIOVANNI ANTONIO CANAL CALLED CANALETTO

1697-1768

Warwick Castle: The South Front

Oil on canvas, 28½ x 47½ inches (72.4 x 120.6 cm.)

Paul Mellon, Upperville, Virginia, 1985

Canaletto painted five pictures of Warwick Castle, two of the east Front and three of the South Front. These were commissioned by Francis Greville, Lord Brooke, who became Earl of Warwick in 1759.

Of the views of the South Front, two remained at Warwick until 1977 when they were sold; one is now in a private collection in America, the other belongs to Baron Thyssen. Our picture was probably painted in London during the winter of 1748-9. Although it is not documented in the Greville collection, its provenance makes it virtually certain that it was there as it later belonged to the Peachey family and Francis's son, George, 2nd Earl of War-wick, married Georgina Peachey in 1771.

Agnew's first bought the picture in 1929; it later belonged to Lord Astor of Hever for whose son we sold it to an American private collector in 1980.

The two views of the East Front were also sold in 1977 and were then bought by Mr. Paul Mellon. However, an objection to their export was lodged and both pictures were eventually bought by the City Art Gallery, Birmingham.

In 1985, our client re-sold this view of the South Front; we bought it and were able to give Mr. Mellon the chance to acquire it, thus providing a happy ending to the story.

RM

Plates 68 (above)

GIOVANNI ANTONIO CANAL CALLED CANALETTO

1697-1768

The Quay of the Dogana

Oil on canvas on panel, 11 X 14³/4 inches (28 x 37.5 cm.)

Private collection, USA, 1988

Plates 69 (below)

GIOVANNI ANTONIO CANAL CALLED CANALETTO

1697-1768

The Piazzetta. SW corner of the Doge's Palace

Oil on canvas on panel, 11 X 14³/4 inches (28 x 37.5 cm.)

Private collection, USA, 1988

It is unusual to find paintings by Canaletto on such a small scale. Although he has allowed himself considerable artistic licence with the topography in each case, the handling is so free and the colour so bright and fresh that this pair perfectly conveys the sunshine and sparkle of the artist's native city.

RM

Plate 70

GIOVANNI ANTONIO CANAL CALLED CANALETTO

1697-1768

Torre di Malghera

Oil on canvas, 12 x 17½ inches (30.5 x 44.5 cm.)

Private collection, USA, 1987

The tower, near Mestre on the Venetian lagoon and a relic of Venetian fortifications dating from the 15th century, was taken down by 1850. In the distance, behind the tower, are the Euganean Hills.

This picture belongs to a group of paintings depicting the area round Padua and the Brenta Canal. These are discussed in a monograph on the artist by W.G. Constable, revised in 1976 by J.G. Links, where they are dated to the mid-1740s and thus shortly before Canaletto came to England. The accents of light here, scattered in small flecks of paint over the picture's sur-face, imbue it with a sense of liveliness while the dark shadows look forward to the romantic feeling that pervades the famous picture of *Old Walton Bridge* at Dulwich.

Canaletto himself etched the subject, which differs only in small details the oil.

The picture belonged to Dmitri Tziracopoulo who owned a most distinguished, small collection of Venetian 18th century paintings in Berlin before the war. Agnew's sold it in 1984 to the Ortiz-Patiño collection and thence again in 1987 to the present owner.

EJ

Plate 71

FRANCESCO GUARDI

1712-1793

Piazza San Marco, Venice

Oil on canvas, 20 x 30½ inches (50 x 77 cm.)

Private collection, 1987

This is a view of the Piazza S. Marco looking west from the south-east corner towards the Church of S. Geminiano (destroyed in the 19th century). The Campanile and the Loggetta are on the left while the centre is occupied by one of the three flagstaffs which held emblems of Venetian provinces. In the background the tower of S. Moise (left) and the church of S. Fantino are visible.

Morassi correctly points out that this is an exceptionally fine work and notes that the unusual composition, in which Guardi places the flag pole at the centre of the picture, is particularly successful. The figures also are full of movement and almost without exception are facing away from the spectator, giving an extra sense of perspective.

RM

Plates 72 and 73

Francesco Guardi

1712-1793

Two Capricci with Ruined Arches

Oil on canvas, each, 19 x 28½ inches (48.2 x 72.4 cm.)

Private collection, USA, 1985

Guardi's *Capricci* are his most personal contribution to landscape, showing him to be at his most inventive when freed from the necessity to produce commissioned views of Venice. Ruined arches, overgrown with vegetation, dilapidated walls and bridges are the stock-in-trade of such pictures but Guardi treats them quite freshly each time. This pair is so full of the spirit of romanticism that one feels that the figures will soon melt away, leaving the now deserted scenes to sink into ruin.

Agnew's bought this pair in 1968 from the collection of Dmitri Tziracopoulo and sold them to a private collection in Scotland, from whom they passed, through us in 1982, to the Ortiz-Patiño collection and thence in 1985 to the present owner, again through Agnews.

EJ

Plate 74

LUIS MELENDEZ

1716 -1780

Cauliflower, Kitchen Utensils and Basket of Food

Oil on canvas, 19 ^{2}/3 x 14^1/2 inches (49.5 x 36.5 cm.)

Private collection, Canada, 1985

In the autumn of 1984 the Meadows Museum in Dallas, which specialises in Spanish painting, organised a fascinating small exhibition of the work of this still-life painter whose work, until then, had been little known and was not very highly regarded except in Spain. The exhibition was a revelation to me and I was delighted to discover that two beautiful pictures in it were likely to come onto the market.

Subsequently I was fortunate enough to be able to find private buyers for both pictures, one of which was this still-life. This painting is the same size as a group of pictures executed for the Royal Palace at the Escorial. Condition is all-important in Melendez' work and here the crispness of handling enables us to admire and to share in the artist's evident delight in describing humble objects in everyday use. At the same time it is the artist's skill in suggesting spatial relationships that makes him one of the great masters of still-life.

RM

Plate 75 (above)

JEAN-BAPTISTE-JOSEPH PATER

1695-1736

Troops halted before a Tavern

Oil on canvas, 10¼ x 15½ inches (26 x 39.4 cm.)

Private collection, USA, 1989

Plate 76 (below)

JEAN-BAPTISTE-JOSEPH PATER

1695-1736

Troops breaking Camp

Oil on canvas, 10¼ x 15½ inches (26 x 39.4 cm.)

Private collection, USA, 1989

This pair, which belonged to Alfred de Rothschild in 1884, are of such high quality that one can readily understand how Watteau, Pater's master, become jealous of his pupil's ability.

Mlle. Ingersoll-Smouse, writing in 1928, was the first art historian to recognise that Pater's work 'demande à êtré étudié avec une érudition minutieuse aussi bien qu'avec du goût' - a claim which is amply illustrated by this pair of 'scenes militaires', painted early in the artist's career. They have a light-heartedness which is quite distinct from Watteau's treatment of similar subjects. Pater prefers to concentrate on the pleasures and diversions of a soldier's life rather than dwelling on its hardships and dangers.

RM

Plate 77

JACOB VAN RUISDAEL

1629-1682

Winter Landscape with Two Windmills

Oil on canvas, 14³/4 x 16¹/2 inches (37.5 x 42 cm.)

Private collection, USA, 1987

Formerly this painting was in the famous Cook collection, Doughty House, Richmond, where it remained until it was bought by Agnew's in 1959. It went to an English private collection until 1986 when it was bought back by Agnew's and sold to the present owner. Its whereabouts were unknown to Professor Seymour Slive when he arranged the great Jacob Ruisdael exhibition at the Mauritshuis and the Fogg Art Museum in 1982, although a small illustration is reproduced in the catalogue.

This belongs to a small group of winter landscapes which dates from the late 1660s to a decade thereafter, Professor Slive assigning our picture to, probably, the late 1670s. This group differs in mood from the dramatic, almost threatening, note to be found in Ruisdael's earlier winter scenes; instead they convey in the most subtle way the silence and stillness, as well as the intense cold, of a winter day. Slive notes that the sunset effect in our picture is unusual, although it occurs also in the Wallace Collection's *Sunset in a Wood*. Here the setting sun seems to be attempting in vain to postpone the onset of darkness.

EJ

Plate 78

REMBRANDT VAN RIJN

1606-1669

St. Peter in Prison

Oil on panel, 23¼ x 18¾ inches (59 x 47.8 cm.)

Joel and Paula Friedland, 1988

Sold in Paris in 1793 by the Comte de Choiseul-Praslin, this picture later belonged to the Prince de Merode in Belgium, for whom we sold it to the present owner.

There are close parallels between this picture, dated 1631, and the *Jeremiah lamenting the destruction of Jerusalem* dated 1630 in the Rijksmuseum.

Although the picture has been known as 'St. Peter penitent' in the past and despite the absence of chains, the straw on the floor and the weak light entering through a small window confirm the setting as a prison.

This painting is one of the artist's earliest and most moving studies of old men.

EJ

Plate 79

JOHN CONSTABLE R.A.

1776-1837

Flatford Mill from the Lock

Oil on canvas, 25 x 35 inches (63.5 x 90.2 cm.)

Private collection, Canada, 1986

This painting, which Constable exhibited at the Royal Academy in 1812 as 'A Water-Mill', disappeared from public view for many years into an American collection from which it reappeared at Christie's on 21 November 1986, when we bought it for the present owners.

At the Constable exhibition at the Tate in 1991 four of the seven sketches connected with this finished picture were shown alongside it. The numerous changes that the composition underwent are described in full in the exhibi-tion catalogue in which a detailed technical report and analysis, by Sarah Cove, also appears. She emphasises how meticulously the finished picture was built up by layer upon layer of small brush strokes, and that Constable's diligent copying of pictures by Claude and Rubens had taught him to adopt compositional devices which create a feeling of space. The result, as the 1991 exhibition catalogue stated, is 'a key work in Constable's early development'.

EJ

Plate 80

Sir Joshua Reynolds P.R.A.

1723-1792

The Yellow Boy, Portrait of Lord George Seymour Conway

Oil on canvas, 24½ x 18¼ inches (62.2 x 46.2 cm.)

Private collection, 1982

In 1770 the Earl of Hertford commissioned Reynolds to paint his seventh and youngest son, George Seymour Conway, then six years old. Reynolds chose to paint him in van Dyck dress, the fashionable attire for the sitters of the time. Although the painting initially recalls Titian's half-length portraits, it is more likely that Reynolds' used van Dyck's famous set of engraved portraits, the *Iconography*, to find a suitable pose for the child. Reynolds' portraits of children are among the most captivating images in his art and the *Yellow Boy* is a particularly brilliant example.

The portrait remained in the family's possession until 1870 when it passed to Richard Wallace, the 4th Marquess of Hertford. It failed to enter the famous Wallace Collection, however, and the family was forced to sell it in 1938 when it was acquired by the King of Roumania. In exile he bequeathed it to his mistress, Madame Lupescu. The portrait was not seen again until 1980 when it was discovered in a bank vault in Mexico City and returned to England where we acquired it.

GN

Plate 81

THOMAS GAINSBOROUGH R.A.

1727-1788

Colonel Norton Knatchbull

Oil on canvas, 91 x 60 inches (231 x 152 cm.)

Private collection, 1987

The sitter was the fourth son of Sir Edward Knatchbull, who was M.P. for Rochester and later Lostwithiel. He married in 1758 Judith Long, and they had one daughter, Frances.

This full-length portrait is one of a splendid group of scarlet-coated officers whom the artist painted in Bath around 1770. They culminated in the magnificent Captain Wade, the Master of Ceremonies in the spa, and Gainsborough invariably set them in charming informal landscapes. Reynolds, with his more formal approach, would have considered a battle scene essential in the background of a portrait of a warrior, but it is typical of Gainsborough's more lyrical vision that he gave his military figures a gentle pastoral setting, which was something he always enjoyed painting.

RK

Plate 82
SIR HENRY RAEBURN R.A.
1756-1823
Mrs Margaret Stewart of Physgill
Oil on canvas, 94 x 60 inches (238.7 x 152.4 cm.)
Private collection, USA, 1989

When the great American collections were being formed, Duveen, the leading art dealer and ace salesman, had the brilliant idea of buying portraits of British aristocrats and selling them to the newly rich in America. In this way some of our greatest British portraits are now in collections such as the Frick in New York and the Huntington Art Gallery in California.

Duveen sold Mrs Stewart's portrait before 1911 to Sir George Cooper, Bart., from whose collection it was bought by Agnew's and sold to the present owner.

The brilliance with which the sitter's silk dress is handled and the painting of her parasol bring Goya strongly to mind.

RM

Plate 83
JOSEPH MALLORD WILLIAM TURNER R.A.
1775-1851
Going to the Ball (San Martino)
Oil on canvas, 24 x 36 inches (61 x 91.4 cm.)
Private collection, USA, 1987

I first saw these pictures, which Turner had exhibited at the R.A. in 1846, in Palm Beach, Florida, in the 1970s when they were in the collection of Sir Harry Oakes' widow. They were later due to be sold at Christie's in New York in 1982, but were withdrawn at the last minute owing to a family dispute; they were re-offered by Christie's in 1984 and then bought in, but, in 1987, Agnew's received them on consignment and sold them to the present owners. The firm had sold them twice previously: in 1895 to Sir Donald Currie and in 1937 on behalf of his grandson, to Knoedler's for Sir Harry Oakes.

The pictures' early history is shrouded in doubt as Turner had exhibited a pair of similar size and titles in 1845 but these had been painted for two different patrons. In 1846 Turner wrote to them both, offering to paint a companion picture for each of them, but not only

Plate 84

JOSEPH MALLORD WILLIAM TURNER R.A.

1775-1851

Returning from the Ball (St. Martha)

Oil on canvas, 24 x 36 inches (61 x 91.4 cm)

Private collection, USA, 1987

confused the titles but put the letters into the wrong envelopes. The upshot of a long story was that all four pictures were returned to the artist. The 1845 pair remained with Turner, and are now in the Clore Gallery (where they have 'Exhibited: 1846' on their frames) as part of the Turner Bequest, and the 1846 pair were sold to Godfrey Windus, one of Turner's biggest patrons at this time.

Although 'San Martino' is a figment of Turner's imagination, there was a Fiesta of Santa Marta concerned with sole-fishing, a subject which would surely have appealed to so keen a fisherman as Turner. This involved brilliantly lit boats with coloured balloons, and a banquet in the Piazza Sta. Marta on the Giudecca which lasted until dawn, so Turner may well have had this in mind when painting *Returning from the Ball*.

RM

Plate 85

WILLIAM DYCE R.A.

1806-1864

Jacob and Rachel

Oil on canvas, 19 x 26 inches (48.4 x 66 cm.)

Private collection, 1983

Dyce's inspiration for this painting arose from his marriage in 1850 to the 19-year-old Jane Bickerton Brand; he was then 44. The subject conveys the artist's expression of joy and optimism at this time. As a critic has written, 'having deferred marriage for so many years [he] chose a subject which constituted the archetype of the Long Engagement scene so popular in the art and literature of the period'. Dyce's religious paintings of the 1840s and '50s are greatly influenced by the work of the German Nazarenes. They also express his own deeply felt religious beliefs. Dyce achieves dra-

matic intensity here by contrasting the emotion of the couple's meeting with the peaceful scene of sheep grazing in the background. This picture originally formed part of the collection of Thomas Miller and his son Thomas Horrocks Miller, Lancashire industrialists, who were clients of Agnew's in the 19th century. Their collection consisted of works by Turner, Bonington and many eminent Victorian painters. At the sale of T.P.Miller's collection at Christie's in 1946 Agnew's bought this picture and handled it in 1983 for the second time in its history.

GN

Plate 86

JOHN FREDERICK LEWIS R.A.

1805-1876

Caged Doves, Cairo

Oil on panel, 30 x 21 inches (76 x 53.5 cm.)

Private collection, Riyadh, Saudi Arabia, 1990

J. F. Lewis is probably the most important of the English Orientalists. He settled in Cairo in 1841 and remained there for 10 years. According to the novelist, Thackeray, who visited him there, Lewis lived and dressed 'like a Turk' and his life-style was that of 'a languid lotus-eater'. His house was near the Great Mosque of Sultan Hassan, and its interior with latticed windows and deep-cushioned divans appears in many of his paintings. The model dressed in Turkish style is his English wife, Marian, whom he married in Cairo in 1847. Lewis produced a large number of detailed drawings and watercolours during his stay in the East and on his return to London began painting a series of 'harem' pictures. The title of this picture, which was exhibited at the Royal Academy in 1864, is allegorical: the fluttering of caged doves symbolises the helplessness of the woman imprisoned in the harem. Ruskin praised Lewis's exoticism when his 'harem' pictures were shown at the Academy and wrote 'Lewis is doing work which surpasses in execution everything extant since Carpaccio'.

GN

Plate 87
Sir Edward Coley Burne-Jones A.R.A.
1833-1898
Pan and Psyche
Oil on canvas, 23⁵/8 x 20⁷/8 inches (59.8 x 51.8 cm.)
Private collection, 1985
(In association with The Lefevre Gallery)

The story of Cupid and Psyche had always appealed to Burne-Jones. His earliest treatment of it dates from the late 1860s when he illustrated William Morris's poem on the myth in *The Earthly Paradise*. In 1869 Burne-Jones began work on this painting but did not complete it until the late 1870s after a tour of Italy with William Morris. The influence of the Italian Quattrocento painters is strongly felt in this picture. The treatment of Pan in particular recalls Piero di Cosimo's *Death of Procris*, which the National Gallery in London had acquired in Florence in 1862, and which would have been familiar to Burne-Jones. This picture was painted for the Greek collector Constantine Alexander Ionides and when sold by him at Christie's in 1897 was purchased by Agnew's for the large sum of 760 guineas. In 1985 we handled this picture for the second time in its history.

GN

Plate 88
SIR EDWARD COLEY BURNE-JONES A.R.A
1833-1898
Portrait of the Baronne Madeleine Deslandes
Oil on canvas, 45½ x 23 inches (109.2 x 55.2 cm.)
Private collection, 1983
(In association with the Artemis Group)

This striking portrait was commissioned by the sitter, Madeleine Deslandes, in 1896, when she was 33. It was exhibited at the Paris Salon the same year. In 1901, after both her marriages had ended in divorce, she took up writing and soon became the centre of an artistic and literary circle that included Oscar Wilde and Maurice Barrès who called her his 'muse juive'. Her novels *Ilse, A Quoi Bon* and *Cruauté* were 'compared to the scent of white lilac or the notes of a violin on a hot night'. Madeleine and her friends were great admirers of Burne-Jones and after the success of his painting *King Cophetua and the Beggar Maid* at the *Exposition Universelle* in Paris in 1889, she persuaded the artist to paint her portrait in the pose of the Beggar Maid. Described as a 'tiny, formidable, blonde Jewish lionne', the Baronne's portrait, which was vehemently criticised at the Salon of 1896, remains an important icon of the Aesthetic Movement.

GN

Chapter 7

GERMANY

CANNING CLAIMED IN PARLIAMENT IN 1826 that he had 'called the New World into existence to redress the balance of the Old'. Today those who write letters to *The Times* about the export of works of art seem to feel that the scales have tipped too far in favour of the New World. This may be so but in practice some things do make the return journey. This applies to the first four major items which I came across when researching this article. Turner's great seascape of *Ostend*, Rubens' *Adoration of the Shepherds*, Burne-Jones' eight-picture cycle of the *Perseus Legend* and Amigoni's portrait of the celebrated castrato singer, *Il Farinelli* - all these were bought by us from North American private collections before we sold them to Munich, Brunswick and Stuttgart respectively. This partial redressing of the balance in favour of the Old World was due to some extent to Germany's remarkable economic recovery in the '60s and '70s, when their museums made many significant purchases. The pre-War years when these museums had been forced by the National Socialists to sell some of their treasures, left a bitter impression, though they reacted with extraordinary resilience. (The consequences of this should be remembered when sales of museum property are proposed here.) In the '80s the escalation of prices made things more difficult for the German museums and in 1989 and 1990 political events have produced further inhibiting factors.

In 1978 for example, we sold one or more pictures to nearly every major museum in West Germany, the von Hirsch sale at Sotheby's coming as the climax of that year, where among other commissions we were able to acquire the *Barbarossa Armilla* for the Germanisches Nationalmuseum in Nuremberg. The £1,100,000 we paid on their behalf was the highest amount ever given at that moment for a non-pictorial work of art, but it was a record we did not hold for long, as nine lots later another 12th century Mosan enamel - the medallion from the Stavelot Retable - was bought for Berlin for £1,200,000.

Things were not quite so active in the last decade, but in 1987 Nuremberg did buy the little bronze lion with the flaming tail which is illustrated on page 181. Münster's watchful eyes rarely miss anything of importance for Westphalia (they had acquired from us one of the missing panels from Koerbecke's *Johannes-Altar* in 1978) and in 1986 they bought the silver-gilt 14th century book cover (Plate 89) which had come from the same source as Nuremberg's fiery lion. In Berlin the Museum für Islamische Kunst, who had already bought one of the beautiful Persian miniatures from the Houghton Shahnameh in the '70s, added a second one in the '80s. Arguably the finest Gaspard Dughet that has ever been through our hands went to the Gemäldegalerie there in 1984 (Plate 90). Known previously as 'A Landscape with an Aqueduct', the scene was identified by Dr. A. N. Zwollo as a *View of Gensano*, and published by Dr. Erich Schleier, who by squatting under a bush of more recent date, was able to locate the position from which it had been painted some 320 years earlier. At the second of our exhibitions of the work of the nonagenarian Lotte Laserstein in 1990, the Deutsches Historisches Museum bought *The Motorcyclist* which had been painted in the German capital in 1928.

Continuing to build up the carefully chosen

Plate 89

WESTPHALIAN, SILVER-GILT, 14TH CENTURY BOOK COVER

15 ¼ x 11 inches (39.8 x 27.9 cm.)

Westfälisches Landesmuseum für Kunst und Kulturgeschichte,

Münster, 1986

group of English pictures which they had started in the '70s, Munich added a fine version of Constable's *Dedham Vale* and Lawrence's elegantly romantic double portrait of *The Talbot Brothers* (Plate 92). Among the various pictures that went to Karlsruhe, three in particular stand out: the lovely *Cows near a River* by Cuyp (Plate 98) and the pair of portraits by Pourbus (Plates 93 and 94), while the outstanding item among other additions to their Kupferstichkabinet was Claude's drawing for the *Enchanted Castle* from the Odescalchi Album (Plate 99). Their neighbours in Stuttgart tend nowadays to concentrate on the 20th century, but did call on our help to secure a newly-discovered portrait by Bernard Strigel (Plate 91) which appeared in Stockholm, and *The Rest on the Flight* (Plate 95) by the Neo-Classical artist Joseph Anton Koch which appeared in London, having been commissioned by the artist's English patron Dr. George Nott. A fine Hubert Robert sanguine of *The Villa Farnese* returned via Agnew's to the Hessisches Landesmuseum in Darmstadt whence it had been wantonly disposed in the '30s. The Niedersächsisches Landesmuseum in Hanover made a major acquisition in Claude's *Pastoral River Landscape* (Plate 96) and an extremely attractive one in their Pittoni *modello* for his altarpiece from the Church of San Giorgio in Brescia (Plate 97).

Finally, it is nice to be able to record that three splendid Turner watercolours, showing *Mainz and Kastel* (Plate 147), *Lurleiberg* and *Wurzburg* went to private collections in Germany. The three wonderful early 16th century drawings illustrated on pages 131 and 133 all came to us in the '80s from a source in Ger-

many. Drawings of this sort are so rare outside the German Print Rooms that the westward journey they made when we sold them, seems to justify the way in which we followed Canning's lead in their case.

The 1980s was the third decade in which I have made annual visits to Germany, and I cannot finish without thanking those kind museum Directors who have always given me such a warm welcome there. Among the many friends I have made, I shall remember with particular affection: in Berlin Dr. Henning Bock and Dr. Erich Schleier; in Bremen Dr. Günter Busch; in Brunswick Dr. Rüdiger Klessmann; in Frankfurt Dr. Margaret Stuffmann and Dr. Michael Maek Gérard; in Hamburg Dr. Werner Hofmann; in Hanover Dr. Hans Werner Grohn; in Karlsrühe Dr. Jan Lauts; in Munich Dr Johann Georg, Prince Von Hohenzollern, Dr Erich Steingräber and Dr. Christoph Heilmann; in Münster Dr. Paul Pieper; in Nuremberg Dr. Kurt Löcher and Dr. Rainer Kahsnitz, and in Stuttgart Dr. Peter Beye and Dr. Gerhard Ewald.

On my initial visit the first person I met was Dr. Horst Vey, who was then working in the Wallraf-Richartz-Museum and we have met annually ever since. His omniscience as a guide and his untiring chauffeuring have given both me and my son Christopher the chance to see much of the wealth of architecture and works of art that lies between the valley of the Lahn and the shores of the Bodensee. To him especially, and to all our friends in Germany, we shall always be very grateful.

DICK KINGZETT

Plate 90

GASPARD DUGHET CALLED GASPARD POUSSIN

1615-75

View of Gensano

Oil on canvas, 38 x 52½ inches (96.6 x 133.5 cm.)

Staatliche Museen Preussicher Kulturbesitz

Gemäldegalerie, Berlin, 1984

Plate 91

BERNARD STRIGEL

1460 - 1528

Portrait of a Nobleman

Oil on panel, 26 x 17 inches (66 x 43.2 cm.)

Staatsgalerie Stuttgart, 1980

Plate 92

Sir Thomas Lawrence P.R.A.

1769-1830

Charles Chetwynd-Talbot, Viscount Ingestre and his brother the Hon. John

Chetwynd-Talbot, sons of the first Earl Talbot

Oil on canvas, 90 x 83 ¾ inches (228.7 x 212.8 cm.)

Bayerische Staatsgemäldesammlungen, 1984

Plate 93

FRANS POURBUS THE YOUNGER

1569-1622

Louis XIII of Austria

Oil on canvas, 39 x 30 inches (99.1 x 76.2 cm.)

Staatliche Kunsthalle Karlsruhe, 1987

Plate 94

FRANS POURBUS THE YOUNGER

1569-1622

Anne of Austria

Oil on canvas, 39 x 30 inches (99.1 x 76.2 cm.)

Staatliche Kunsthalle Karlsruhe, 1987

Plate 95 (above)

Joseph Anton Koch

1768-1839

The Rest on the Flight

Oil on panel 12 x 16 ¼ inches (31.7 x 41.5 cm.)

Staatsgalerie Stuttgart

1981

Plate 96 (below)

Claude Gellée called le Lorrain

1600-82

Pastoral River Landscape

Oil on canvas, 16 ¾ x 21 ¼ inches (42.5 x 54 cm.)

Hannover Niedersächsisches Landesmuseum, Landesgalerie

Stiftung Kommerzienrat Georg Spiegelberg, 1984

Plate 97

Giambattista Pittoni

1687-1767

Madonna and Child with Saints

Oil on canvas, 21 x 12 ¼ inches (53 x 31 cm.)

Hannover Niedersächsisches Landesmuseum, Landesgalerie

Stiftung Kommerzienrat Georg Spielgelberg, 1986

Plate 98

AELBERT CUYP

1620-91

Cows near a River

Oil on panel 18 ½ x 29 inches (47 x 73.7 cm.)

Staatliche Kunsthalle Karlsruhe, 1986

Plate 99

CLAUDE GELLÉE CALLED LE LORRAIN

1600-82

Enchanted Castle

Pen and brown wash, 7¼ x 13¾ inches (18.2 x 34.5 cm.)

Staatliche Kunsthalle Karlsrühe, 1983

Chapter 8

JAPAN

AGNEW'S FIRST VENTURE INTO THE Japanese market goes back to 1968. A group of dealers and auctioneers, sponsored by what was then the Board of Trade, and welcomed by the British ambassador, visited Tokyo and arranged for exhibitions and sales to be held in the following year. Agnew's first exhibition was at the prestigious Mitsukoshi department store in Tokyo, and was followed by other shows at the same venue. Through these exhibitions we established contact with a number of museums and dealers, and some important sales were made.

In 1987 a major policy decision was made to visit the country on a regular basis and to deal as far as possible directly with the purchasers of works of art rather than through intermediaries. Almost immediately the benefits of this change of approach appeared, and as a result a considerable number of important works of art has passed through Agnew's to Japan. Initial problems for the inexperienced traveller were soon overcome; what to do about an embarrassing hole in a sock at a formal and shoe-less Japanese lunch, how to get to an obscure address in Osaka which even a taxi driver could not find, how to eat noodles dipped in raw egg with chopsticks. More important was the stimulating challenge of doing business in a new environment, in an unfamiliar language and above all of attempting to foster a change of taste in Japanese interest in western art. The great Japanese collections of the 1920s, Matsukarta, Ishibashi and O'Hara, mainly formed in Paris and on the advice of western and Japanese artists, fixed a canon for Japanese taste which has varied very little from that time. Based on

an interest in French painting of the Impressionist and Post-Impressionist eras and in the Ecole de Paris, this taste remained fixed for a period of over 50 years. With the development of Japanese industrial power and wealth, evidenced by a dramatic rise in the purchasing power of the yen, this taste not only dominated Japanese collecting throughout the '80s but, from the time of the 1986 sale at auction of van Gogh's *Sunflowers* to a Japanese insurance company, was the major factor in the world art market. Spiralling prices for such paintings created a flow of art from the hitherto predominant USA to Japan: a 'bubble market' which culminated in the sale of two such pictures for record prices in excess of $70 million each in the summer of 1990. That such excesses held within them their own seeds of destruction was already clear to many participants in the art market, even at the time they took place, and was clear to those in Japan who were more interested in the long-term aesthetic values of their collecting than the profits of short term speculation. To these clients the merits of buying European paintings of an earlier date, free from the vagaries of fashion and the pressures of speculative money, were already becoming clear before the market itself went into reverse in the summer of 1990 and made the point obvious to the world in general.

During this period, the National Museum of Western Art in Tokyo, for many years a client of Agnew's, added further to their collection the van Dyck portrait of the *Marquis of Leganés* (Plate 101) and the Tiepolo sketch of the *Apotheosis of Admiral Vettor Pisani* (Plate 100). Leganés, described by Rubens as 'one of the

Plate 100

GIOVANNI BATTISTA (GIAMBATTISTA) TIEPOLO

1696-1770

The Apotheosis of Admiral Vettor Pisani

Oil on canvas, 16 ¼ x 28 ½ inches (41 x 72 cm.)

The National Museum of Western Art, Tokyo, 1989

Plate 101

SIR ANTHONY VAN DYCK

1599-1641

Marquis of Leganés

Oil on canvas, 87³/₄ x 51³/₄ inches (223 x 125 cm.)

The National Museum of Western Art, Tokyo, 1988

greatest connoisseurs of this age', was an extraordinary collector; at his death in 1655 he owned no fewer than 20 Rubenses, 11 Titians, five Velasquez and numerous van Dycks. This portrait, probably painted in 1634, is a splendid example of the artist's formal portrait style. The Tiepolo, a sketch for the ceiling fresco in the Palazzo Pisani-Moretta in Venice, shows the introduction into heaven of a distinguished number of the Pisani family, an admiral who takes his place among the gods of Olympus, including Jupiter, Mars and, appropriately for a great sailor, Venus Anadyomene, born of the sea. It is a typical example of the artist's mastery of light and airy space.

The Tokyo Fuji Art Museum, a new Agnew's client, purchased two major 17th century European paintings, Frans Hals's *Portrait of a Bearded Man* (Plate 103) and the Georges de la Tour *The Smoker* (Plate 102) as well as the beautiful small Turner *Seascape with a Squall coming up* (Plate 106). Interest in such English landscapes of the 18th and 19th centuries was a major element in Japanese buying over the period covered in this book, an interest in landscape in general being perhaps part of a much older Japanese taste as shown in its indigenous art forms, further stimulated by major exhibitions of Turner and Constable during the 1980s. The Shizuoka Prefectural Museum, from whose steps there is a fine view of Mt. Fuji, is making a collection of European landscape painting, and added to an outstanding Turner watercolour the Claude *Pastoral Landscape* (Plate 108), a Gaspard Dughet, a Constable sketch and an exceptional Gainsborough landscape in coloured chalks (Plate 136).

Two other fine Turner watercolours passed into Japanese private collections (Plates 146 and 154). Another anonymous client purchased from Agnew's, through Marlborough Fine Art Tokyo, the full-length Reynolds portrait of the *Countess of Eglinton* (Plate 104), a picture which in the 1920s might well have found a home in the Frick or Andrew Mellon collections but in an age when such portraits are no longer fashionable, required a discerning buyer from a totally different culture to appreciate its merits.

The new Japanese taste for things English was shown to extend into the late 19th century with the sale of the large sketch for Burne-Jones' last masterpiece, the *Sleep of Arthur in Avalon* (Plate 107) and the magnificent Albert J. Moore *Revery* (Plate 105).

In contrast to this new-found interest in European Old Masters and English paintings, it has been a particular pleasure for Agnew's to be able to bring to the Bridgestone Museum of Art, one of the best-known and most prestigious of the traditional Japanese collections, two pictures of exceptional quality from the French 19th century, the Daumier *Don Quixote* (Plate 110), the artist's first treatment of this subject with which he was so fascinated, and the Boudin *Plage à Trouville* (Plate 109).

Agnew's have begun to build in Japan a long-term relationship with a number of important clients. As Japanese taste develops towards an even wider variety of western art, we anticipate a growing interest in and knowledge of the highest quality Old Master and British paintings which we are able to offer to them.

JULIAN AGNEW

Plate 102

GEORGES DE LA TOUR

1593-1652

The Smoker

Oil on canvas, 27½ x 24¼ inches (70 x 62 cm.)

Tokyo Fuji Art Museum

Plate 103

FRANS HALS

1581/5-1660

Portrait of a Bearded Man

Oil on canvas, 40 ¼ x 35 ½ inches (102 x 89.5 cm.)

Tokyo Fuji Art Museum

Plate 104

SIR JOSHUA REYNOLDS P.R.A.

1723-92

Jane, Countess of Eglinton

Oil on canvas, 94 x 54 inches (239 x 137 cm.)

Marlborough Fine Art Ltd., Tokyo, 1988

Plate 105

ALBERT J. MOORE A.W.R.S.

1841-1893

Revery

Oil on canvas, 46 x 29 ½ inches (117 x 75 cm.)

Private collection, 1990

Plate 106

J.M.W. TURNER R.A.

1775-1851

Seascape with Squall Coming Up

Oil on canvas, 18 x 24 inches (46 x 61 cm.)

Tokyo Fuji Art Museum

Plate 107

SIR EDWARD COLEY BURNE-JONES A.R.A.

1833-98

The Sleep of Arthur in Avalon

Gouache, 23½ x 77½ inches (60 x 197 cm.)

Marlborough Fine Art Ltd., Tokyo, 1989

Plate 108

CLAUDE GELLÉE CALLED LE LORRAIN

1600-82

Pastoral Landscape with Piping Figures

Oil on canvas, 39$^1/_2$ x 52 inches (99.7 x 133.3 cm.)

Shizuoka Prefectural Museum of Art, 1990

Plate 109

EUGENE BOUDIN

1824-98

Scène de Plage aux Environs de Trouville

Oil on canvas, 14 x 22½ inches (35.5 x 57 cm.)

Bridgestone Museum of Art, Ishibashi Foundation, 1991

Plate 110

HONORÉ DAUMIER

1808-79

Don Quixote et Sancho se rendant aux noces de Gamaches

Oil on canvas, 15 ½ x 12 ¼ inches (35.5 x 57 cm.)

Bridgestone Museum of Art, Ishibashi Foundation, 1991

Chapter 9

AUSTRALIA

DURING THE 1970s, AGNEW'S HELD A number of highly successful exhibitions in Australia, both in Sydney and in Melbourne. The philosophy behind these ventures was that in a country with a population of predominantly European origin and of considerable potential wealth, there would emerge in time a group of collectors who would be active in the areas of European and English works of art. As a result of these exhibitions, two private collectors did indeed purchase the major parts of their collections from Agnew's; furthermore the state art galleries with whom we had had close connections for many years, increased their activity dramatically and made important additions to their collections. However, when a new group of Australian collectors appeared in the early 1980s, their interest lay predominantly in the Impressionist and Post-Impressionist fields and in Australian art rather than in earlier European painting, and their preferred method of collecting was through the saleroom rather than through dealers. After a hectic outburst of purchasing, problems in the Australian economy meant that by the end of the decade many of these collectors had already ceased to be active in the market, and in some cases their recently-formed collections have already been dispersed.

These same economic problems have considerably limited the purchases of the national and state museums during the 1980s but we are able to illustrate two important paintings which have gone from Agnew's to, respectively, the Australian National Gallery in Canberra and the National Gallery of Victoria in Melbourne. Jacopo di Cione, the youngest brother of Orcagna, painted the Canberra altarpiece in 1367 (Plate 111); the hieratic composition is enriched by the rich decorative detail of the robes of the saints and the canopy surrounding the throne.

The Canaletto, *Bacino di San Marco from the Piazzetta* (Plate 114), one of a series of four paintings commissioned from the artist by the English collector William Holbech for his dining room at Farnborough Hall, Warwickshire, is a unique example of this particular view, the architecture being enlivened by the varied activities of the market place in the foreground.

Amongst private collectors, James Fairfax, for many years an Agnew's client and a connoisseur of great taste, has added to his select group of Old Master paintings and drawings the jewel-like van Mieris *Cavalier* (Plate 112), the romantic Amigoni of *Bacchus and Ariadne* (Plate 113), and two of the finest French 18th century drawings to come on the market during the decade: the Watteau, *Three studies of a young man* (Plate 124), formerly in the John Nicholas Brown collection and the Fragonard, *Rinaldo in the garden of Armida* (Plate 128), notable both for its scale and its extraordinary state of preservation. In a typical gesture, he has recently announced that he is to give the collection over a period of years to the Art Gallery of New South Wales in his home town Sydney, a gift which will transform the galleries of European paintings there and begin to close the gap between that collection and its traditional rival in Melbourne. Such a demonstration of public-spirited generosity can only serve to advance the cause of the arts throughout Australia.

JULIAN AGNEW

Plate 111

JACOPO DI CIONE

active 1365-98

Madonna and Child Enthroned with Saints

Oil on panel, 22 x 11 ½ inches (55.9 x 29.2 cm.)

Australian National Gallery, Canberra, 1987

[127]

Plate 112 (above)

FRANS VAN MIERIS

1635-81

A Cavalier

Oil on panel, 7½ x 5¾ inches (19 x 14 cm.)

Collection of James Fairfax, 1988

Plate 113 (below)

JACOPO AMIGONI

c.1682-1752

Bacchus and Ariadne

Oil on canvas, 36 x 53¾ inches (51 x 61 cm.)

Collection of James Fairfax, 1985

Plate 114

Giovanni Antonio Canal called Canaletto

1697-1768

Bacino di San Marco

Oil on canvas, 51 ½ x 65 inches (132 x 165 cm.)

National Gallery of Victoria, Melbourne, Felton Bequest, 1985 (E01/1985)

Chapter 10

OLD MASTER DRAWINGS

On June 22nd 1891, Agnew's purchased, at the sale of Miss James's collection of Old Master drawings at Christie's, eight Watteau drawings for a four figure sum. 100 years later, in 1991, the one Watteau drawing we had in stock sold for more than 200 times that amount. The steady rise of drawing prices in the last century has accelerated dramatically over the last decade and has radically altered the market. Once the province of museums and collectors with rather cerebral taste, drawings suddenly became a fashionable commodity for a new breed of private collector and prices soared as major masterpieces appeared on the market.

The major event in the Old Master drawing world in the 1980s was the sale of Old Master drawings from Chatsworth at Christie's in the summer of 1984. Collected mainly by the 2nd Duke of Devonshire (1672-1729), the Chatsworth collection is the most important in this country. Prices for drawings were transformed overnight; in just over two hours 70 drawings sold for over £21 million. A sheet by Mantegna became the first drawing at auction to exceed a million pounds, although this record was overtaken a few minutes later by the Raphael which made over £3 million. The most acquisitive buyers at the sale were relatively new to the market. Of the museums, private collectors and dealers, the most important newcomer was the Getty Museum. The Getty had bought their first drawing in 1981 when they acquired a Rembrandt red chalk study of *Cleopatra*. By 1988 however, when they published their first catalogue of *European Drawings*, they had acquired 200 sheets. In this period, as John Walsh points out in his introduction, they concentrated on buying the rarest material, mainly from the Italian and German Renaissance.

The Chatsworth sale and the arrival of the Getty on the drawing scene undoubtedly revolutionised the market. Suddenly more attention was given to drawings; they became 'fashionable'. As more drawings came on to the market worldwide, more drawing exhibitions were staged and more dealers sprang up. More collectors invaded the market, some for pleasure, some for investment. During this period the British Museum mounted over 10 major drawing exhibitions, from *Raphael* in 1983 to *Guercino* in 1991. We handled a greater number of drawings at this time than at any other in our history. As a new departure, we mounted a series of drawings and sculpture exhibitions which proved extremely successful. In 1982 we organised a show of *Claude Drawings and Paintings* and in 1986 staged *From Claude to Géricault* in which we showed French paintings, drawings and works of art. The majority of the drawings illustrated in this short article were not purchased at auction but were acquired privately, and most were acquired abroad. Again, in numerical terms, we sold approximately half the drawings illustrated to museums either in this country or abroad.

In 1982 we acquired from a private source in Germany three 16th century drawings in an almost perfect state of preservation. They were designs for stained glass by three artists who had trained in Dürer's workshop around 1504: Hans Baldung, Hans Schäufelein and Georg Pencz. The beautiful Baldung of *A Monk Preaching* (Plate 115), sold by us to the Getty Museum in 1982,

Plate 115

HANS BALDUNG GRIEN

c.1484/5-1545

A Monk Preaching

Pen and brown ink and black chalk

12⅛ x 8¹³⁄₁₆ inches (30.8 x 22.3 cm.)

Collection of the J. Paul Getty Museum, Malibu, California, 1983

was seen for the first time at the great *Hans Baldung Grien* exhibition in Karlsruhe in 1959 and is among the earliest drawings by the artist, described as Dürer's most gifted pupil. The second drawing in the group which dates from the first decade of the 16th century, Schäufelein's *Scenes from the Life of St Andrew* (Plate 116), was acquired by the Pierpont Morgan Library. Schäufelein was an artist not previously represented in the Library's small but prestigious collection of early German drawings. The third drawing is the elegant *Study for a Stained-Glass Window* (Plate 117) by Georg Pencz, and was also acquired by the Getty Museum. Unlike the drawings of Baldung and Schäufelein, who never ventured abroad, Pencz's design reveals the influence of Italian Renaissance painters on German artists at this period. Pencz visited Northern Italy in 1529 and may have seen Giulio Romano's recently completed frescoes in the Palazzo del Tè in Mantua.

In 1977, we had organised the exhibition at Agnew's of *Old Master Drawings from Holkham*, the first time the drawings had been seen publicly for almost 30 years. In 1986 we were instrumental in the sale to the National Gallery, Washington, of the famous Raphael cartoon from Holkham, *The Madonna and Child with Saint John the Baptist* (Plate 118), a study for the painting, known since the 18th century as *La Belle Jardinière*, in the Louvre. Few full-scale cartoons from the Renaissance have survived and those that do, like this, provide a remarkable insight into artists' working methods at the beginning of the 16th century. The Holkham cartoon, last shown in the *Raphael Exhibition* at the British Museum in 1983, was celebrated for its mysterious and haunting beauty from the moment it entered the collection of the 1st Earl of Leicester at Holkham in the 18th century. The second Raphael drawing handled by us at this time was the *Study for the Disputa* (Plate 119) from the Loyd Collection, acquired by the Getty Museum in 1984. In the 1920s it was found, unattributed, in an album of drawings at Lockinge House by the famous connoisseur A.G.B. Russell, who recognised it as being from Raphael's hand. The drawing is connected with one of Raphael's most important commissions, the decoration of the Vatican *Stanze* which he was working on from 1509 to 1511.

Another drawing from the Loyd Collection entrusted to us for sale in the early 1980s was Poussin's *A Dance to the Music of Time* (Plate 121) which was acquired by the National Gallery of Scotland in 1984. Formerly in the collections of the two great French connoisseurs Pierre Crozat and Pierre-Joseph Mariette, this is one of Poussin's finest drawings and the only surviving study for a painting. The picture, dated c.1640, is now in the Wallace Collection, London. It was commissioned by Cardinal Giulio Rospigliosi, later Clement IX; the symbolism of the subject is that 'Poverty is converted to riches by work; riches lead to pleasure which can lead again to poverty, if indulged in to excess'. It was from this picture that Anthony Powell took the title of his series of novels.

Poussin and Claude rank as the two most outstanding French draughtsmen of the 17th century. In 1981, in association with E.V. Thaw, we acquired from an American collector over 50 drawings by Claude from the famous Odescalchi Album and in 1982, to mark the artist's tercentenary, we organised an exhibition of his paintings and drawings in which we showed 30 sheets from this album: landscape and figure drawings, animal studies and compositional studies for paintings. The album has a fascinating history. During his lifetime Claude greatly prized his own drawings and rarely parted with them. It is possible that the Odescalchi Album was assembled by the artist's heirs for sale to Queen Christina of Sweden, an important patron and collector who was living

Plate 116 (left)

HANS LEONHARD SCHÄUFELEIN

1480?-1538/40

*Design for a Stained Glass Roundel with Scenes from the
Life of St. Andrew*

Black pen on pale yellow paper

11⅝ x 10⁷⁄₁₆ inches (29.5 x 26.5 cm.)

Signed with monogram 'S.H.' above a little shovel

The Pierpont Morgan Library, New York, 1982 (1982.89)

Plate 117 (right)

GEORG PENCZ

c.1500-1550

*Study for a Stained-Glass Window with the Coat of Arms of
the Barons von Paar (recto)*

Study for a Sceptre with the initials M.B. (verso)

Pen and brown ink and grey wash (recto)

Black chalk (verso)

Diameter, 9¹¹⁄₁₆ inches (24.7 cm.)

Collection of the J. Paul Getty Museum, Malibu, California, 1983

Plate 118

RAFFAELLO SANZIO DA URBINO, CALLED RAPHAEL

1483-1520

The Madonna and Child with Saint John the Baptist

Black chalk with traces of white chalk, outlines pricked for transfer

$36^{15}/_{16}$ x $26^{3}/_{8}$ inches (93.8 x 67 cm.)

National Gallery of Art, Washington, 1986. Purchased with funds from the Armand Hammer Foundation.

Plate 119

RAFFAELLO SANZIO DA URBINO, CALLED RAPHAEL

1483-1520

Studies for the Disputa (recto)

Pen and brown ink, 12 ¼ x 8 ³⁄₁₆ inches (31.2 x 20.8 cm.)

Collection of the J. Paul Getty Museum, Malibu, California, 1984

in Rome at that time. By 1713 the album was owned by Don Livio Odescalchi and remained in the Odescalchi family for over 200 years. It originally contained 80 drawings representing over 40 years' work. The earliest drawing which we illustrate here is the beautiful *Group of Trees in Sunlight* (Plate 120) dated 1633 and the latest is *Philip baptising the Eunuch* (Plate 122) dated 1677. Within the confines of 'landscape' there is a great variety of subject matter. We can almost see the artist at work and follow him as he sketches on the Palatine or when he escapes the city to draw the beautiful landscape of the *campagna*. We were delighted that both American and European museums and private collectors were able to acquire sheets from this great album and that several pages found homes in private collections in France, the artist's native country.

In the 1980s major exhibitions devoted to French artists were staged in Paris and New York: *Claude* in 1982, *Watteau* in 1984, *Boucher* in 1986 and *Fragonard* in 1987. In the same decade more French material came on to the market as the number of auctions in Monte Carlo, Paris and the French provinces increased. At this time we handled several major French drawings of the 18th and 19th centuries. The earliest, Watteau's elegant *Study of Three Male Figures* (Plate 124), came from the collection of John Nicholas Brown. The Brown family, of Providence, Rhode Island, were successful in many fields - shipping, banking, manufacturing, railroads and land speculation. Born in 1900 John Nicholas Brown was described as 'the world's richest baby', when he inherited 10 million dollars as an infant. After graduating in art history at Harvard, Brown inherited a further 20 million dollars and in the 1920s formed a great collection of Old Master drawings as well as drawings by contemporary artists such as Matisse and Picasso. Brown bought a number of his drawings from Richard Owen, a dealer

active in London and Paris and famous for his taste in French and Italian 18th century drawings. The Watteau, Trinquesse and Guardi, which we illustrate here (Plates 124, 126 and 133), all come from the Brown collection and were purchased from Owen in the 1920s.

At this same period we handled two very important Fragonard drawings: the powerful *Bull entering a Stable* (Plate 127) which came from the collection of Casimir Stralem, and *Rinaldo in the Garden of Armida* of 1761 (Plate 128). Both sheets illustrate very different aspects of Fragonard's art and imagination. The latter drawing had not been seen by the public for almost 100 years when it appeared on the market in 1990, and its condition was impeccable. In the 19th century both drawings had belonged to the same distinguished French collector, the Marquis de Biron.

The Guardi *Studies of Fishing Boats* (Plate 133) from the Brown collection is one of three important Venetian 18th century drawings which we acquired in the 1980s. This extremely rare and beautiful study of barges, or *bragozzi*, dates from the late 1760s or 1770s and is related to the group of boats in one of Guardi's most famous paintings, the *Punta di Dogana* in the Wallace Collection. As James Byam Shaw writes of these drawings, 'the pen seems to flutter over the paper like a winged insect hardly confined to earth and produces by its very inconstancy a magical effect'. Giovanni Battista Tiepolo's *Madonna and Child with St. John the Baptist* (Plate 132) comes from the famous Orloff Album which was sold in Paris in 1920. The album, assembled by a Russian dilettante, Gregory Vladimirovitch Orloff (1777-1826), contained 96 drawings by Tiepolo, several of which are large, highly finished presentation drawings such as this one.

In 1986 we organised an exhibition entitled *From Claude to Géricault, The Arts in France 1630-1830*, in which we showed another important

Plate 120

CLAUDE GELLÉE CALLED LE LORRAIN

1600-1682

A Group of Trees in Sunlight

Pen and brown wash, 9¾ x 7½ inches (24.8 x 19 cm.)

Private collection, 1982

Plate 121 (above)

Nicolas Poussin

1594-1665

A Dance to the Music of Time

Pen and brown ink and brown wash

5¹⁵⁄₁₆ x 7¹³⁄₁₆ inches (14.8 x 19.8 cm.)

National Gallery of Scotland (Department of Prints and Drawings) 1984

Plate 122 (below)

Claude Gellée called le Lorrain

1600-1682

Philip Baptising the Eunuch

Pen and brown wash

8¹⁄₁₆ x 11½ inches (20.5 x 29.2 cm.)

Private collection, France 1989

Plate 123

CLAUDE GELLÉE CALLED LE LORRAIN

1600-1682

Wooded Landscape

Black chalk, brown wash on paper tinted red

8⅛ x 11⅛ inches (20.7 x 28.3 cm.)

Private collection, New York, 1984

Plate 124

JEAN-ANTOINE WATTEAU

1684-1721

Study of Three Male Figures

Red chalk, 8⅛ x 6⁷⁄₁₆ inches (20.6 x 16.4 cm.)

Collection of James Fairfax, 1989

Plate 126 (below)
LOUIS-ROLAND TRINQUESSE
1746-1800
Study of a Lady of Fashion
Red chalk, 22½ x 17¼ inches (57.2 x 43.8 cm.)
The Pierpont Morgan Library, New York. The Von Bulow Fund.
1990 (1990.16)

Plate 125 (above)
GABRIEL DE SAINT-AUBIN
1724-1780
Study for an Allegory of Archaeology (recto)
Study of a Statue of Diana (verso)
Red, black and blue chalks, pen and brown ink, brown, grey
and yellow wash heightened with white (recto)
Black chalk, pen and brown ink (verso)
8½ x 5¾ inches (21.6 x 14.6 cm.)
Trustees of the British Museum, 1985

Plate 127

JEAN HONORÉ FRAGONARD

1732-1806

Bull Entering a Stable

Black chalk, brush and brown wash on cream paper

$9^7/_8$ x $9^7/_{16}$ inches (25.1 x 24 cm.)

Private collection, 1984

drawing we had acquired in France: Greuze's large preparatory figure study for one of his most famous paintings, *L'Accordée du Village* (Plate 131), exhibited at the Salon of 1761 and now in the Louvre. In the same exhibition we showed Ingres' incisive drawing of *Admiral Sir Fleetwood Broughton Pellew* (Plate 129). Ingres drew this portrait in Rome in 1817 when the sitter was 28. Ingres' portrait drawings of English visitors to Rome are some of the most fascinating of his creations. Agnes Mongan has written: 'Ingres must have found the English enormously interesting for he scrutinised them with care...he saw the infinite variations in their looks yet was able to record and make visible the national characteristics which distinguished them'. The essential traits of Pellew's character, self-esteem, arrogance and ambition, so sharply observed in this portrait, were later to put an end to his naval career.

In 1989 we acquired a beautiful portrait drawing by Ingres' pupil, Chassériau, the most important drawing by the artist to have come on the market in the last 10 years. Ingres predicted that his precocious young pupil, who had entered his studio at the age of 12, would be 'le Napoléon de la peinture'. His portrait drawing of *Raymond de Magnoncourt* of 1851 (Plate 130) was drawn only five years before the artist's premature death at the age of 37. The sitter, who was 16 at the time, reclines in a graceful attitude of *rêverie mélancolique* and personifies the *vague à l'âme* of the French Romantics. The portrait drawings of Ingres and Chassériau have been compared by Anita Brookner, who concludes that Chassériau's portrait drawings 'even

Plate 128

JEAN HONORÉ FRAGONARD

1732-1806

Rinaldo in the Garden of Armida

Black chalk and brown wash, 14 x 18⅛ inches (35.5 x 46 cm.)

Collection of James Fairfax, 1991

at their most finished, have a softness that is not necessarily Romantic but at least indicative of a less uncompromising attitude to the model, of a more poetic approach to human beings'.

Like Ingres and Chassériau, Degas and Helleu were also contemporaries. In 1982 we bought an exceptional pastel by Helleu which we subsequently sold to a private collector, the *Symphonie en Blanc, Yvonne Paulmier* (Plate 134). The setting is the artist's studio and the Louis XVI *canapé* on which the model is seated appeared in the posthumous sale of Helleu's collection at the Hôtel Drouot in Paris in 1928. Whereas Helleu enjoyed and found inspiration in fashionable society and was mainly influenced by Whistler and Sargent, Degas sought his inspiration among the young *ouvrières*, the ballet dancers,

laundresses and milliners. Degas' obsession with the dance began in the 1870s and continued until the end of his life. This ravishing *Study of a Dancer* (Plate 135), which was bought by the artist's brother René at the *Vente Degas* in 1918, is a preliminary sketch for the dancer resting in one of his most famous paintings, *The Dance Class at the Opéra* of 1872 in the Musée d'Orsay. A classic image, it illustrates perfectly the artist's claim that 'The dancer is only a pretext for drawing'.

The 1980s began with the Chatsworth drawings sale; the 1990s with the sale of drawings from Holkham. The art of the dealer is to discover the masterpiece. We hope to unearth many more master drawings in the future.

GABRIEL NAUGHTON

Plate 129 (left)
JEAN-AUGUSTE-DOMINIQUE INGRES
1780-1867
Portrait of Admiral Sir Fleetwood Broughton Reynolds Pellew
Pencil, 12 x 8¾ inches (30.5 x 22.3 cm.)
Private collection, New York, 1989

Plate 130 (right)
THÉODORE CHASSÉRIAU
1819-1856
Portrait of Raymond de Magnoncourt
Pencil heightened with white chalk
85/8 x 1013/16 inches (22 x 27.5 cm.)
Collection of Jaime Ortiz-Patiño, 1989

Plate 131

JEAN BAPTISTE GREUZE

1725-1805

Study for l'Accordée du Village

Black and red chalks heightened with white on buff paper

16¾ x 17⅛ inches (42.6 x 43.5 cm.)

Collection of Jaime Ortiz-Patiño, 1986

Plate 132

GIOVANNI BATTISTA TIEPOLO

1696-1770

Madonna and Child with John the Baptist

Pen and brown ink and brown wash

16¾ x 11½ inches (41.5 x 29.2 cm.)

Collection of Jaime Ortiz-Patiño, 1985

Plate 133

FRANCESCO GUARDI

1712-1793

Studies of Fishing Boats

Pen and brown ink, black chalk and wash

10 ⅝ x 17 ⁵⁄₁₆ inches (27 x 44 cm.)

Collection of Jaime Ortiz-Patiño, 1986

(In association with David Tunick, Inc.)

Plate 134

PAUL HELLEU

1859-1927

Symphonie en Blanc, Yvonne Paulmier

Pastel, 62¼ x 70¼ inches (159 x 178.5 cm.)

Private collection, 1983

Plate 135

EDGAR DEGAS

1834-1917

Dancer Seated, Study for Dance Class at the Opéra

Essence and pencil on pink paper

10¾ x 8¼ inches (27.3 x 21 cm.)

Collection of Mr & Mrs Eugene Victor Thaw, New York, 1986

(In association with David Tunick, Inc.)

Chapter 11

WATERCOLOURS

WATERCOLOURS ARE WITHOUT DOUBT the most stable section of the whole art market. Supplies are plentiful for all but the half dozen or so rarest artists, prices are still very reasonable, and many buyers accumulate drawings steadily over a long period and are replaced, in due time, by a younger generation of collectors. Dealers' exhibitions and auction sales attract a great many visitors, some of whom are thereby encouraged to begin collecting themselves. All of this leads to a steady demand in a market that is very largely based in Britain, supported by some serious American collectors. At present there are only a few buyers in Europe, although their numbers are slowly increasing. However, most recently the Japanese have begun to collect watercolours with a special liking for Turner as will be evident from the illustrations which follow. Indeed the provenances of the drawings described in this chapter do indicate that some have travelled far and wide.

Our annual watercolour exhibitions (1992 was the 119th), which have become such a popular fixture in the calendar, continued to be extremely successful during the period under review, with sales averaging 70 - 75% of 200 - 230 watercolours (80% in 1987 and 257 drawings in 1984).

In 1984 we had a second barrel to our watercolour gun: in May we held an exhibition of Mrs. Cecil Keith's collection. Her father, J. Leslie Wright, had given his large collection of watercolours to the City Art Gallery, Birmingham, and apart from a very few bequests, all the other 100 items in the exhibition were for sale. As Hope Keith was well known in the watercolour world, and had always welcomed visitors at her home in Rusper, Sussex, there was tremendous keenness among collectors to acquire something from the exhibition with the result that 91% was sold. Museums were particularly active buyers, and included the British Museum, the Fitzwilliam, the Tate, the Bolton Museum, and the Whitworth Art Gallery. But most of Hope's friends managed to acquire something they had long coveted in her house so that the venture was a resounding success.

In 1987 Andrew Wyld joined Agnew's after running his own gallery for 15 years, first in Cork Street and then in Clifford Street. He now heads our watercolour department, and has introduced some improvements in the annual watercolour exhibitions: first by postponing the opening from late January until March in the expectation of better weather and secondly, from 1990 onwards, by reducing the numbers hanging in the top gallery to about 100 of the most important drawings with a subsidiary hang downstairs of moderately priced items which do not appear in the catalogue and can thus be taken away at the time of purchase.

Selecting the watercolours for illustration here has not been easy as the choice was so wide, but we have aimed above all to record the outstanding examples while at the same time suggesting the variety of drawings that we have handled.

The notes on the individual drawings in this chapter have been divided between Andrew and myself, and those who fancy that they can sort out which parts of 'Monro School' drawings were done by Turner and which by Girtin will no doubt be able to tell his hand from mine.

EVELYN JOLL

Plate 136

THOMAS GAINSBOROUGH R.A.

1727-1788

A Wooded Landscape With Horses Drinking

Black, white and coloured chalks on grey-blue paper,

9⅛ x 11½ inches (23.2 x 29.2 cm.)

Shizuoka Prefectural Museum of Art, Japan, 1990

Dated 'Mid to later 1770s' by John Hayes, the first recorded owner was Herbert Horne who sold it to Edward Marsh in 1904; it later belonged to the distinguished drawings collector John Nicholas Brown of Providence, Rhode Island from whose collection we bought it.

The drawing is unusual in the variety and brilliance of the coloured chalks employed - blues and pinks - which give the surface an extraordinary feeling of vibrancy.

Plate 137

THOMAS GAINSBOROUGH R.A.

1727-1788

Riders near a wooded pool

Black chalk and watercolour, 8 $^7/_8$ x 12$^1/_2$ inches (22.5 x 31.6 cm.)

Private collection, 1984

Dated by John Hayes 'mid to later 1780s' and thus 10 years later than Plate 136. The first owner was Guy Bellingham Smith, who made a fine collection of Gainsborough landscape drawings. It later belonged to J. Leslie Wright and then to his daughter Mrs Dorian Williamson who bequeathed it to her sister Mrs Cecil Keith; it was sold by Agnew's from her collection in 1984 to a private collector in America who resold it through Leger's in 1989.

Described by Hayes as 'a superb late drawing', he draws attention to Gainsborough's 'unerring application of wash in defining shape'. Gainsborough's handling here is seen at his sketchiest and yet most assured, resulting in one of his most romantic and brilliant drawings.

Plate 138

THOMAS JONES

1742-1803

Ruins of Maecenas' Villa and the Villa D'Este at Tivoli

Pencil and watercolour, 11¼ x 16⅞ inches (28.8 x 42.9 cm.)

The Art Institute of Chicago, 1988

Jones spent much of November 1777 staying in Tivoli and sketching in the surrounding country-side. He records in his diary:

'10th Went to see the Villa D'Este...an immense production of Art.'

'16th Here are the superb ruins of Mecenus' villa and other antique edifices...This country like that of the Latin's seems formed in a peculiar manner by Nature for the study of the Landscape Painter...At Tivoli - the foaming Torrents rush down the Precipices into the deep Abyss with a fearful Noise and horrid Grandeur - The immense Masses of Stone rise abrupt - luxuriantly fringed with Shrubs, and crowded with antique towers and Temples.

(Memoirs of Thomas Jones 'The Walpole Society' Vol. 32 (1946-48) pp.65-67.)

Plate 139
JOHN ROBERT COZENS
1752-1797
The Small Temple at Paestum
Watercolour, 10 x 14½ inches (25.3 x 37 cm.)
The Whitworth Art Gallery, The University of Manchester, 1984

Three acquisitions (Plates 139, 140 and 141) added substantially to the Whitworth's already magnificent collection of Cozens' work which had been further augmented in 1973 by the purchase of the seven sketchbooks that Cozens used on his visit to Italy in 1782-3 with his millionaire patron William Beckford, the first owner of these three watercolours. They were dispersed at Beckford's sale in 1805 and later belonged to various members of the Agnew family.

Cetara is based on a sketch dated 29 September 1782 and *Paestum* on one almost certainly done on 7 November that year.

In all three watercolours, Cozens shows his extraordinary skill at capturing the *genius loci* of his subjects. In the drawing of Rome, the dome

Plate 140

JOHN ROBERT COZENS

1752-1797

St. Peter's from the Villa Borghese

Watercolour, 10⅛ x 14⅝ inches (25.7 x 37.1 cm.)

The Whitworth Art Gallery, The University of Manchester, 1984

PLATE 141
JOHN ROBERT COZENS
1752-1797
Cetara. A Fishing Town on the Gulf of Salerno
Watercolour, 10¼ x 14¾ inches (26 x 37.3 cm.)
The Whitworth Art Gallery, The University of Manchester, 1984

of St. Peter's, glimpsed at sunset and framed between the trunks of two umbrella pines, provides a wonderfully romantic image, while the temple at Paestum, starkly silhouetted against the pale sky, conjures up a vision full of associations with the classical world.

The view of *Cetara*, taken from the sea, is dominated by the mountains behind. The clouds above, which echo the shapes of the peaks, add to the impression of their height, thus dramatically dwarfing the fishing port below.

These three examples reinforce A.J. Finberg's view that Cozens' best work possesses a haunting beauty that is 'spiritual not material', a judgement put still better by Constable who said that Cozens' art was 'all poetry'.

Plate 142

Thomas Girtin

1775-1802

Jedburgh Abbey from the South East

Watercolour over pencil with slight touches of bodycolour

16 $^5/_8$ x 21$^3/_4$ inches (42.3 x 55.4 cm.)

Private collection, 1991

Girtin is known to have visited Jedburgh, just north of the Scottish border, in 1796, when he made a pencil sketch of the village (now in the British Museum); part of the British Museum sketch provided the basis for the watercolour of 1800 which is now in the National Gallery of Scotland, Edinburgh. This watercolour, like ours, was once owned by Sir John Ramsden (4th Baronet). It thus seems probable that *Jedburgh Abbey from the South East*, which was commissioned by the first Baronet, was likewise completed in 1800.

Girtin was clearly moved by the drama and beauty of the location, and produced at least four finished watercolours of the subject apart from ours and that at Edinburgh.

Plate 143

JOSEPH MALLORD WILLIAM TURNER R.A.

1775-1851

The Lake of Thun

Watercolour, $10^7/_8$ x $15^1/_2$ inches (27.7 x 39.3 cm.)

Private collection, USA, 1986

(In association with The Leger Galleries)

Painted for Turner's most important patron in the first half of his career, Walter Fawkes (1769-1825), it later belonged to Norman D. Newall, whose distinguished collection was sold at Christie's in December 1979. It reappeared in the New York saleroom in 1985 bought by Agnew's and Leger's and was sold by the latter to the present owner in 1986.

It is based on two pencil sketches in Turner's 'Lake Thun' sketchbook in use on his visit to the Continent in 1802. These sketches are extremely slight and demonstrate that even this early in his career Turner needed only the merest jottings (a hairline squiggle indicates the streak of lightning) as an *aide-memoire* when it came to producing finished watercolours.

There is also a print of the subject in the *Liber Studiorum* series, published in 1808. The print depicts a later stage as the storm has already broken and the surface of the lake is lashed by white horses whereas, in the watercolour, the composition is dominated, and the impending storm thus only heralded, by the flash of lightning.

Usually dated c.1806, close affinities with the British Museum's *Lake Brienz*, which is dated 1809, suggest that *The Lake of Thun* may have been painted a year or two later than 1806.

Plate 144

JOSEPH MALLORD WILLIAM TURNER R.A.

1775-1851

Mount Blanc, from Fort Roch, in the Val d'Aosta

Watercolour, $26^3/_8$ x $39^3/_8$ inches (67 x 100 cm.)

Makepeace Investments Ltd, 1984

This watercolour was painted for Walter Fawkes, sold by the Rev. Ayscough Fawkes at Christie's in 1890 and bought by Agnew's for Sir Donald Currie. It descended to his granddaughter, from whom Agnew's bought it in 1984.

It is based on a watercolour study on grey paper, originally a page from the 1802 'St. Gothard and Mont Blanc' sketchbook. The study is now in the Fitzwilliam Museum.

Turner introduces some figures, not in the study, into the composition which can be dated 1805-10. Three girls are shown looking in awestruck wonder into the gorge, and he emphasises the height of the precipice by placing a waterfall behind. The heroic scale matches the grandeur of the scenery in this 'sublime' example which marks Turner's complete emancipation from the 18th century topographical tradition.

Plate 145
JOSEPH MALLORD WILLIAM TURNER R.A.
1775-1851
Poole, Dorset with Corfe Castle in the Distance
Watercolour, heightened with touches of bodycolour
5½ x 8½ inches (14 x 21.9 cm.)
Private collection, England, 1990

In 1811 William Bernard Cooke commissioned Turner to work on the *Southern Coast* series, a project which was to cover the coast from Whitstable in Kent as far westwards as Watchet in Somerset. Turner made two tours, in 1811 and 1813, to gather material for the series, which was mainly engraved by the brothers William and George Cooke. *Poole,* which can be dated c.1812, was one of the first three subjects to be engraved in 1814. Turner was originally engaged to make 24 drawings for the series.

The view is taken from Canford Heath looking towards Poole, with Brownsea Island just visible on the extreme left. *Poole,* which is exceptionally well-preserved, is one of the gems of a series in which Turner demonstrates fully for the first time his mastery in depicting immensities of distance in drawings of very modest dimensions. The cool colours of the landscape are bathed in warm sunshine, investing the scene with a radiance unmatched in Turner's work before this.

The first owner of *Poole* was Charles Stokes, Turner's stockbroker. Since then it has passed through Agnew's hands in 1869, 1874, 1909 and 1989.

Plate 146
JOSEPH MALLORD WILLIAM TURNER R.A.
1775-1851
Scarborough
Watercolour with scraping-out, 11½ x 15⅞ inches (26.6 x 40.4 cm.)
Private collection, Osaka, Japan, 1988

Scarborough was a favourite subject of Turner's. This watercolour differs in mood from earlier treatments. While they show the sea, flat calm and some way off in a scene like a film-still, here a stiff breeze whips the waves into white crests which sparkle in the sunshine. The two girls at the water's edge are as graceful as any figures in Turner's entire output.

Owned by the Agnew family from 1900-1979 we then sold it to an American collector who lent it to the Turner exhibition in Japan in 1986. This was no doubt a factor, when it returned to Agnew's for sale in 1988, in it being bought by a Japanese collector.

Plate 147

JOSEPH MALLORD WILLIAM TURNER R.A.

1775-1851

Mainz and Kastell

Watercolour, with some body-colour

8¼ x 14⅜ inches (20.8 x 36.5 cm.)

Private collection, Germany, 1987

Bought from the artist by his friend and patron Walter Fawkes of Farnley Hall, Yorkshire, this watercolour remained at Farnley until 1912 when bought by Agnew's; when we sold it to a collector in Germany in 1987 it was the fourth time the drawing had been through our hands.

Turner visited Mainz at the end of August 1817 and tradition has it that he sold the celebrated series of 51 Rhine watercolours to Fawkes on his arrival at Farnley on 15 November, but it is much more likely that he completed the set while staying there.

However, this drawing differs from the others in the series in three important ways: first it is larger than any of the others, secondly

it is unique in being on white paper instead of the paper being prepared with a grey wash and thirdly it is more freely handled, having much in common with the limpid drawings of Venice done in 1819. These factors, coupled with the fact that 50 seems a more likely number for a set of drawings than 51, suggests that *Mainz and Kastell* may have been added to the Fawkes group later in 1819-20 when Turner was making some rather larger Rhine drawings for Sir John Swinburne, Fawkes' neighbour.

A further point of interest is that Turner's finger prints are visible in the sky above the rowing-boat, introduced there no doubt to produce the particular textural effect he desired.

Plate 148

JOSEPH MALLORD WILLIAM TURNER R.A.

1775-1851

Ullswater

Watercolour, 13 x 16³/₄ inches (33 x 42.6 cm.)

Private collection, USA, 1986

Engraved in 1835 for the series *Picturesque Views in England and Wales*, *Ullswater* went to America in 1910 and was brought to England in 1973 by Brian Pilkington from whom Agnew's bought it in 1984 and sold it to the present owner.

The *England and Wales* series gave Turner the opportunity to depict a wide range of scenery in all kinds of weather, a challenge to which he responded magnificently. That *Ullswater* was among the six *England and Wales* subjects chosen for the Turner exhibition in Paris in 1983-4 confirms its reputation as one of the very finest of this superb series.

Although famous for depicting images of disaster such as fire and shipwreck, Turner was equally masterly at portraying the tranquil face of nature as *Ullswater* proves. The scene is one of utter stillness, not a ripple disturbs the surface of the lake, while the impression of a hot, windless summer's day is enhanced by the violet and purple hues on the hills in the distance.

PLATE *149*

JOSEPH MALLORD WILLIAM TURNER R.A.

1775-1851

Margate Beach

Watercolour and bodycolour on buff brown paper

8½ x 11½ inches (22.2 x 29 cm.)

Private collection, USA, 1987

A page from a sketchbook of Margate subjects bought by Ruskin from Mrs. Booth, 'Turner's good Margate housekeeper'. Ruskin subsequently broke up the sketchbook and this sheet was either sold by him or given to Charles Eliot Norton (1827-1902), the first Professor of the History of Art at Harvard; more recently it belonged to Ray Murphy, whose collection was dispersed at Christie's in 1986 when *Margate Beach* was bought by Agnew's and sold to the present owner.

An article by Edward Yardley in *Turner Studies* attempts to reassemble the sketchbook and suggests that it was used 'exclusively for what are almost certainly *plein-air* studies for which Turner used a variety of media'. He suggests a dating of 1835-40 and notes that at least one page is stained with raindrops, thus supporting the theory that Turner was sketching out-of-doors.

Turner was a frequent visitor to Margate. This watercolour, showing a stretch of wet sand in the foreground, with a line of surf and the outlines of a jetty beyond, and storm clouds over the horizon, contains elements that recur in a number of similar sketches. To each, however, Turner brings a freshness of vision that stamps them with his own particular magic.

PLATE 150

JOSEPH MALLORD WILLIAM TURNER R.A.

1775-1851

Venice: A Storm Approaching San Giorgio Maggiore and the Dogana

Watercolour on paper prepared with a pale grey wash

$8^5/_8$ x $12^5/_8$ inches (22 x 32 cm.)

Private collection, USA, 1986

(Courtesy of Sotheby's Inc., New York)

Virtually unknown until the Turner Bicentenary Exhibition in 1974-5, this superb watercolour was sold at Christie's in March 1982 and bought by Agnew's on behalf of John R. Gaines who in 1986 resold it at Sotheby's in New York, where it was bought by the present owner.

On Whatman paper watermarked 1834, this watercolour seems firmly assigned to the 1840 visit and belongs with three others, all depicting storms. The most dramatic is this drawing where the lurid reds of the sky contrast with the pale green buildings of S. Giorgio and the Dogana, all ghostly-white, seen through a veil of mist or rain as the storm sweeps in from the lagoon. On the right are gondolas which Shelley described thus: 'I can only compare them to moths of which a coffin might have been the chrysalis'.

PLATE 151
JOSEPH MALLORD WILLIAM TURNER R.A.
1775 - 1851
Lausanne from Le Signal by Moonlight
Watercolour and pencil, 9 x 13 inches (22.8 x 33 cm.)
Mr Helmut Stern, Ann Arbor, Michigan, 1988

As Turner visited Switzerland for four years in succession from 1841-4 it is not easy to date the drawings done on these trips, with accuracy. But Andrew Wilton's suggestion that this drawing belongs to 1841 seems convincing. Another watercolour of the same title and size, but from quite a different viewpoint, is in an English private collection.

Our drawing belonged at the beginning of this century to W.G.Rawlinson who catalogued Turner's prolific work for engraving. In 1917 we bought it from him and sold it to R.A. Tatton; in 1965 we bought it again and sold to Mrs Dorothy Edinburgh of Chestnut Hill, Massachusetts; it was sold by her children in New York in 1987 where we bought it once more and sold it to the present owner in 1988.

Turner's technical skill and delicacy of touch are brilliantly displayed here: the gradation of colour from the darks in the foreground to the light tones in the distance is managed with the utmost economy and subtlety. At the same time Turner directs our eyes, by making the plume of smoke curl up towards the focal point of the composition, the surface of the lake turned to silver by the light of the moon.

PLATE 152

JOSEPH MALLORD WILLIAM TURNER R.A.

1775-1851

The Lauerzersee with Schwyz and the Mythen

Watercolour, with pencil, pen and red ink and scratching out

$8^7/_8$ x $11^1/_4$ inches (22.6 x 28.6 cm.)

Private collection, England, 1991

This watercolour was given by Turner to Mrs Booth, his mistress and housekeeper in Chelsea. In 1909 it was sold by Agnew's to Walter Jones whose Turner watercolours included both the 'Blue' and the 'Red' Rigis; on 11 April 1991 it was sold anonymously at Sotheby's (77) and bought by Agnew's for the present owner.

The view is taken looking westwards across the lake towards Schwyz, with the twin peaks of the Mythen towering above it. In the past, the drawing has been incorrectly identified both as 'Lake Lucerne' and as 'A View on the Rhine'.

It almost certainly dates from Turner's trip to Switzerland in 1843 when his itinerary is known to have included Schwyz.

By this stage in his career, Turner had achieved complete mastery in watercolour, using a great variety of techniques coupled with an extraordinary rapidity of execution which, as the sureness of touch with the pen shows here, in no way appears hurried. What are unusual are the very vivid colours, not only blues and ochres but also quite strong greens, a colour only occasionally favoured by Turner.

Plate 153

JOSEPH MALLORD WILLIAM TURNER R.A.

1775-1851

Pallanza, Lago Maggiore

Watercolour, 14½ x 21½ inches (36.8 x 54 cm.)

Shizuoka Prefectural Museum of Art, Japan, 1986

The identification is uncertain and both Lake Thun and Bellinzona have been suggested; if the latter is correct then the water must be read not as a lake but as a river, the Ticino.

Andrew Wilton dates this drawing 1848-1850, and he suggests that it, like *Florence* (Plate 154), belongs to the final set of watercolours that Turner was still working on at his death, although he points out that it is exceptional in the series as having no figures in the foreground. Although there are signs in some of

Turner's work at this very late date of his failing powers due to age, *Pallanza* completely refutes this suggestion and is indeed 'the strongest and most vigorous of the group,' as Wilton notes.

Pallanza's first owner was L.B. Mozley; at his sale at Christie's in 1865 it was bought by Agnew's and sold to Sir John Fowler; at his sale in 1899 we bought it on behalf of Sir Donald Currie; it descended to his great grand-daughter for whom we sold it in 1986 to the present owners.

Plate 154

JOSEPH MALLORD WILLIAM TURNER R.A.

1775-1851

Florence

Watercolour and pencil, 13⁷⁄₈ x 21⁷⁄₈ inches (35.4 x 54.3 cm.)

Mr Susumu Ônishi, Japan, 1990

Never exhibited until shown in our watercolour exhibition in 1990, this drawing had entered the Hosmer collection in Montreal in 1896 and remained there until 1960 when it passed into the possession of a private collector in the US for whom we sold it to Japan.

Andrew Wilton dates *Florence* c.1850-1, one of Turner's three final watercolours. He suggests that it may belong to a final set of 10 drawings that Turner was working on when he died and which was intended to follow the three series already completed in 1842, 1843 and 1845. If so, Wilton sees this as re-affirming Turner's 'constant concern with the finished watercolour that can be seen as the most consistent and central medium of communication for him in his entire life's work'. Wilton also notes that *Florence* and the other two final watercolours *Genoa* and *Lake Thun* have in common, 'unusually large figures placed on an elaborate platform which occupies the foreground of the design'. At the same time the distances in each case are exceptionally evanescent so that it may not be fanciful to suggest that Turner has here deliberately chosen to dissolve the landscape in light and mist, conscious, as surely he was, that his own life was ebbing away.

Plate 155

JOHN MARTIN

1784-1854

Kilmeny

Pencil, watercolour, gum arabic and oil paint, 21½ x 32⅛ inches (63.6 x 81.5 cm.)

Private collection, USA, 1988

This work as an early intimation of such achievements of Martin's maturity as *The Plains of Heaven*, now in the Tate Gallery, which was completed 20 years later. The source for the distant view on the right of the composition is the valley of the River Wye, a subject treated by the artist in a number of watercolours painted in the 1840s.

Although exhibited in the 1940s as *The Plains of Calypso* the composition is certainly Martin's contribution to the Society of British Artists in 1833 (no. 742), where it bore the title *Kilmeny*. The catalogue entry includes a long passage from 'The Queen's Wake' by James Hogg, which begins:

'They bore her far to a mountain green,
To see what mortal had never seen;
And they seated her high on a purple sward,
And bade her heed what she saw and heard...'

and concludes with the lines:

'Kilmeny sighed and seemed to grieve,
For she found her heart to that land did cleave.'

Martin exhibited the picture again in 1837, at the New Society of Painters in Watercolours (no. 124), with by the same lines of verse.

Plate 156

SAMUEL PALMER

1805-1881

The Eastern Gate

Watercolour and body colour with pencil and scratching out

19³/₄ x 27¹/₂ inches (50 x 70 cm.)

Signed: Samuel Palmer, lower left and bearing a label attached to

backboard inscribed: *No. 1./The Eastern gate, from "L'Allegro"./Right*

against the Eastern gate,/Where the great sun begins his state,/ Robed in

flames and amber light,/The clouds in thousand liveries dight;/While the

ploughman, near at hand,/Whistles o'er the furrowed land,/And the

milkmaid singeth blithe,/The mower whets his scythe,/ And every shepherd

tells his tale/Under the hawthorn in the dale./Samuel Palmer/Furze Hill

House,/Mead Vale, Red Hill/Surrey.

Private collection, UK, 1988

Completed in the last year of the artist's life, this watercolour illustrates John Milton's poem *L'Allegro*, lines 59-68.

A chalk and wash study for *The Eastern Gate* is in the collection of the Victoria and Albert Museum. It is probably also the design on which the etching *The Early Ploughman* (Lister 9) was based.

Leonard Valpy, John Ruskin's solicitor, shared Samuel Palmer's life-long interest in the work of John Milton, and this work is one of a group illustrating *L'Allegro* and *Il Penseroso* that he commissioned during the 1860s.

Plate 157
DAVID COX
1787-1859
Lancaster: Peace and War
Watercolour over pencil heightened with bodycolour and scratching out
19¼ x 29¼ inches (48.5 x 74.5 cm.)
The Art Institute of Chicago, 1990

This watercolour depicts a view across a valley to Lancaster Castle with the mountains of the Lake District in the distance beyond Morecambe Bay. In the foreground, a shepherd boy and a girl watch a troop of soldiers and their baggage waggons marching past.

Cox's interest in portraying the relationship between the peaceful elements of the countryside and the spectre of war stems from drawings he worked on whilst staying at Seabrook near Hythe, Kent in 1838. There, he conceived the idea of painting Lympne Castle with accompanying soldiers and rustics, a subject he exhibited in 1848 as *Peace and War*, (*Society of Painters in Water-Colour*, 1848, no. 154, now in the Lady Lever Art Gallery, Port Sunlight). In the early 1840s he transferred the scene from Lympne to the altogether grander setting of Lancaster Castle and its surrounding countryside when he executed the present watercolour.

Plate 158

PETER DE WINT

1784-1849

The Dingle at Badger, Shropshire

Watercolour, 17½ x 24 inches (44.5 x 61 cm.)

Private collection, 1987

Some of de Wint's most important patrons lived in Shropshire. In particular, the Cheneys, who lived at Badger near Bridgnorth, patronised the artist, and at least one member of the family was his pupil. Three watercolours of *'The Dingle'* were included in the artist's studio sale at Christie's in 1850.

This watercolour, which dates from the early 1840s, shows de Wint's technique at its most appealing: a fully loaded brush sweeps straight across the paper combining speed with a sureness of touch that was his especial contribution to the medium. Also the colours here are unusually rich and varied.

[173]

Plate 159 (above)

JOHN RUSKIN

1819-1900

The Garden of San Miniato, Florence, 1845

Watercolour and bodycolour, 13⅛ x 15⅝ inches (33.3 x 47.3 cm.)

The National Gallery of Art, Washington, 1991

Plate 160 (below)

THOMAS SHOTTER BOYS

1803-1874

The Pont Royal and the Tuileries from the Institut, Paris

Watercolour, 9¾ x 13⅞ inches (24.8 x 35.3 cm.)

Private collection, 1990

Plate 161

WILLIAM DYCE

1806-1864

Pegwell Bay

Watercolour, 9³/₄ x 13³/₄ inches (24.7 x 34.9 cm.)

Aberdeen Art Gallery, 1990

Dyce, who was born in Aberdeen and trained in Rome, later settled in London. In 1857 and 1858 he and his family went to Kent for their holiday and this watercolour is inscribed 'Oct '57'. It later served as a study for what is perhaps the finest and certainly the best known painting by Dyce, *Pegwell Bay. A Recollection of October 5 1858,* which the artist exhibited at the Royal Academy in 1860 and which is now in the Tate Gallery.

In the watercolour, which lacks the figures that appear in the oil, Dyce was evidently concentrating his attention on the pebble-strewn beach and the chalk cliffs behind it.

Pegwell Bay lies between Ramsgate to the north and Sandwich to the south. The watercolour's first owner was Sir John Pender who had a distinguished collection of British pictures including Millais' *The Proscribed Royalist;* at the Pender sale in 1897 the Dyce was bought by Sir George Agnew and descended in his family until we sold it in a private treaty sale to Aberdeen.

Chapter 12

THE ALGARDI BUST

THE STORY OF THE ALGARDI BUST, AS IT came to be known, was a particularly difficult and distressing episode in the history of Agnew's. A major quarrel with the export review committee, unfavourable newspaper articles, questions in the House of Commons and a prosecution of the company at Bow Street magistrates court; such experiences were far from the usual pattern of our dealings in the art market. But ultimately Agnew's position was fully vindicated and all allegations of wrong-doing refuted.

The cause of all this uproar was a marble bust of an Italian cleric, Antonio Cerri, by the 17th century baroque sculptor Alessandro Algardi. Art-historically, Algardi is known as the principal rival, in Rome, of the young Bernini, though his rather austere and classical style was soon supplanted by the more exuberant and vigorous work of his younger rival, who secured all important papal patronage for his far-reaching sculptural and architectural schemes. Nevertheless Algardi was a refined and subtle artist and the bust of Monsignor Cerri is a delicate and psychologically revealing work of art. Probably created shortly after 1635, the bust may have been intended for a tomb and indeed a copy of it was later placed in the sitter's funerary chapel in the Church of the Gesù in Rome. The bust probably came to England early in the 19th century and was acquired in 1917 for the collection of Mrs Walter Burns, the sister of the American collector J.P. Morgan. It was from her house at North Mymms Park that it was sold by auction on 24 September 1979.

Up until that year Agnew's had had only occasional dealings in the field of sculpture but with the arrival of William Agnew, a sixth generation descendant of the original Thomas, a new specialist department was set up. During his apprenticeship at Christie's William had been partially responsible for the cataloguing of the North Mymms sculpture and had been impressed by the quality of the Algardi, as indeed we all were when we went to inspect it before the sale. However, the opening estimate for its value far exceeded any amount we had put aside for the new department and, after failing to secure a commission bid from a California museum, it was only a chance conversation with the American dealer Eugene Thaw that revealed a possibility that we might revive our initial idea of bidding for the bust in partnership with him. As the auction date approached it became increasingly clear that not only was the bust of great aesthetic value and art-historical importance but also that competition to buy it was likely to be lively. To increase the level of our potential bid we decided to bring in the London dealers Artemis, of which Eugene Thaw was vice-chairman, as a third partner in our bidding syndicate. On the morning of the sale William and I sat in the marquee outside the house as the bust was brought to the rostrum, ready to bid to a level of £200,000. Competition was vigorous up to £145,000 but after a single bid of £150,000, Jo Floyd, the chairman of Christie's, knocked down the lot to Agnew's. We returned to London happy with our purchase, if a little apprehensive of the consequences of our bold entry into the field of sculpture.

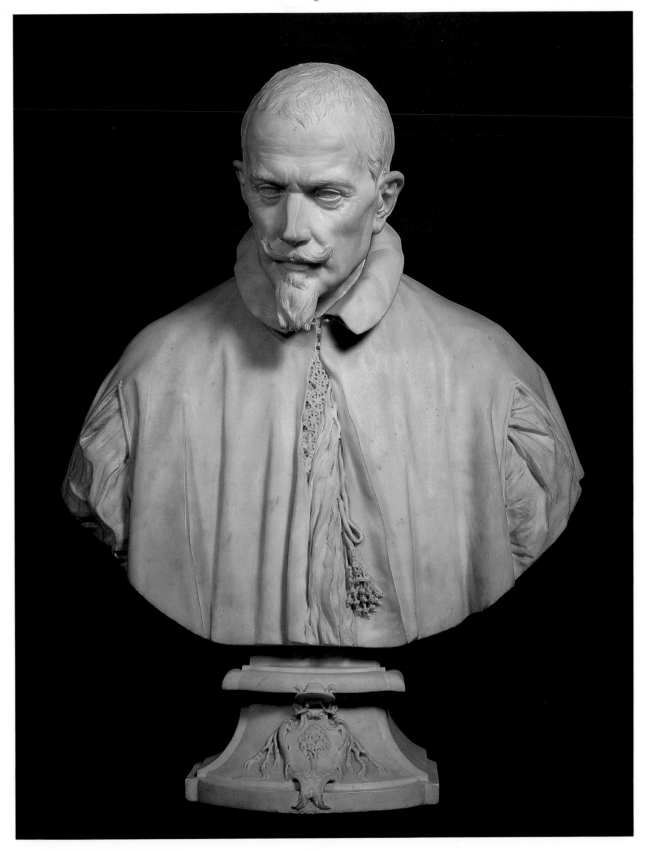

Plate 162

ALESSANDRO ALGARDI

1598-1654

Bust of Monsignor Antonio Cerri

White Marble, 33 inches (85.5 cm.) high.

Manchester City Art Galleries, 1981

The next day it appeared that any apprehensions were groundless. A trustee of the Metropolitan Museum in New York appeared in the gallery, even before the bust arrived, and asked for a reserve on it for the museum. Within hours an agent for the under-bidder, revealed as the San Francisco Museum, came in to register his client's further interest. The next day Timothy Clifford, the director of Manchester City Art Gallery, appeared with the news that his gallery had bid for the bust; was it still available? Clearly we had bought a sculpture for which the major museums of the world were ready to compete. After consultations amongst ourselves, we decided to ask a price of £265,000 (representing the purchase price of £165,000, including the 10% buyer's premium, plus a profit of £100,000 for the three partners), with the first offer to the Metropolitan as we had promised to the trustee, but keeping the other interested parties informed (the number having now grown to three to include an Italian museum). Within weeks the bust was submitted to the trustees of the Metropolitan, the director comparing both object and the price to the Warwick Vase, which had recently been acquired by the museum, and the purchase was approved.

Immediately we applied for an export licence, and our application was, not surprisingly, referred to the Export Reviewing Committee. When the meeting took place, most of it was devoted to art-historical arguments as to whether the bust was of sufficient aesthetic merit to warrant delaying the granting of an export licence. There was some limited discussion of the sale to the Metropolitan Museum and of the price, but it was a complete surprise to me when at the conclusion of the meeting, the chairman of the committee announced not only that the bust was considered to fall within the necessary art-historical criteria but also that the price, for the purpose of an offer from a museum in the UK, should be reduced to £200,000. Such a recommendation was quite unprecedented. Never before, when an arm's-length open market sale of an object had been agreed, had the Committee ever attempted to reduce the sale price; indeed, were it to do so, the whole system by which an owner is fully compensated for the retention of a heritage object in the UK, would be destroyed. Immediately after the meeting we protested in the strongest possible terms to the Minister for the Arts (to whom the Committee reports) against this extraordinary recommendation. Although the proceedings of the Committee are meant to be confidential within a few hours the recommendation to reduce the price had been leaked to the newspapers, perhaps by some interested party. Clearly the issue was to become a matter of public controversy.

To what extent this was to be so we had not at this stage yet appreciated. But within a few weeks, further newspaper reports suggested that our partnership bid for the bust had been illegal and the whole affair took on an added dimension. The point at issue was whether we had infringed the laws designed to prevent the 'ringing' of auctions, a form of conspiracy to keep down the price, by not declaring our partnership, (in fact our partnership bid had had the effect of raising the price) before the auction. Immediately we issued a public statement pointing out that far from dissuading anyone to bid at the auction (an essential part of a 'ring's' operation), we had combined to make a bid that otherwise would not have been made, and thus raised the price. In spite of this, the issue was raised in the House of Commons by an MP who had long been interested in the auction laws, though more usually in their application to Welsh cattle auctions, and who asked that the affair should be referred to the Attorney General to consider whether a prosecution should be brought. Finally the matter was put into the hands of the police to whom we explained the whole story. But in the meantime the Minister for the Arts refused to accept or reject the controversial recommendation from the Reviewing Committee and the eventual destination of the bust remained unresolved.

It took the best part of a year for the authorities to make a decision as to what to do, but eventually they announced that a test case was to be brought in an attempt to clarify an obscure area of the auction laws. Much of the pressure to do so came from the chairman of the Reviewing Committee who believed that he had revealed a conspiracy to deceive the Committee and to export the bust at an artificially high price. Within a few minutes of the case's opening, the weakness of the prosecution was quickly revealed by our able defence counsel, and when it became clear that no single one of the partners had had any intention to bid on their own account, the case to all intents and purposes collapsed. The magistrate's judgement entirely vindicated our position and exonerated us completely from the charges. The Minister for the Arts was able, through an ingenious formula, to confirm the sale price of £265,000 without appearing to contradict the Committee. In a rather bitter atmosphere, the money to retain the bust was raised and the situation finally resolved.

In retrospect, very little that was positive came out of this sorry episode. Within a short period the chairman of the Reviewing Committee came to the end of his appointment, and his successors have never attempted to vary the price of any work of art where a definite sale has taken place. The necessity for joint-share partnerships among dealers has increased as prices in the art market have risen, and there has been no clarification of the obscure and outdated auction laws. And the Algardi bust rests in lonely state in the Manchester City Art Gallery, the only Italian baroque sculpture in a collection of predominantly English paintings.

JULIAN AGNEW

Chapter 13

SCULPTURE AND WORKS OF ART

IT IS NOT WIDELY KNOWN THAT AGNEW'S DEAL in sculpture, as the general public thinks of us as Old Master, English picture and water-colour dealers. We have, however, been dealing in sculpture and works of art for a very long time, advertising as early as 1876 in our Waterloo Place catalogues that we were 'open daily for the exhibition and sale of modern paintings, water colour drawings...bronzes, statuary, rare porcelain and works of art generally'. We have in recent years held specialist exhibitions. The first, in 1981, was devoted wholly to sculpture, and the second and third, in 1985 and 1989, exhibited sculpture and Old Master drawings together. This combination suits our galleries, with their rich burgundy wall-covering, perfectly, and re-creates a taste admired by collectors since the period before the War. Dealers such as Elizabeth Drey and David Peel and well-known collectors such as Baron Hatvany and Paul Wallraf, all active in these fields in the 1950s and 1960s, would have felt perfectly at ease in recent years in our galleries admiring a Renaissance bronze or a drawing by Tiepolo.

We have also had dealings with some of the most famous collections of works of art formed recently, such as that of the Swiss industrialist Ernest Kofler-Truninger. Kofler-Truninger formed an impressive group of medieval ivories, enamels and metalwork which, before it was split up and sold, was one of the finest of its kind in private hands. The market has seen new records established for medieval works of art

when, for example, the von Hirsch collection was dispersed by Sotheby's in 1978. In the field of medieval metalwork, von Hirsch, another Swiss, concentrated on German enamels while Kofler-Truninger built up a fine group of French *chasses*. Another notable collection to come to the market in recent years was the Ernest Brummer collection of medieval enamels dispersed by Spink's in collaboration with Galerie Koller in Zurich in 1979.

In this context a particularly attractive metalwork sculpture from the Kofler-Truninger group was sold by us to the Germanisches Nationalmuseum, Nuremberg, in 1987. The sculpture, Mosan or North Saxon, of a seated lion (Plate 163) appears to be an *aquamanile* - a vessel used to hold water for the washing of hands. It would have, in fact, been originally positioned in the centre of a candelabrum and this image can often be seen in the paintings of Northern European artists such as Dirk Bouts or Rogier van der Weyden. A less ornate six branch candelabrum can be seen in van Eyck's celebrated *Arnolfini Marriage* in the National Gallery, London. The sculptor of our bronze has also deliberately modelled the lion's tail to appear as though it were on fire. It is because of this that ours and several other related examples are known as *Flaming-Tailed* or *Flammenschweiflöwen* bronzes.

While the Kofler-Truninger collection was researched and published in full in the 1960s, it is unusual to find collections of sculpture

Plate 163

MOSAN OR NORTH SAXON

c.1400

Lion

Brass, 7¼ x 6¾ inches (18.5 x 17 cm.)

Germanisches Nationalmuseum Nürnberg, 1987

recorded in this way. It is therefore common to rely on auction catalogues of famous collections such as the marbles from Wilton or Thomas Hope's collection assembled at Deepdene in the 19th century. When a white marble relief of *Dido of Carthage* (Plate 164) appeared in a small auction in Dorchester in the Spring of 1988 it generated considerable excitement at Agnew's before the sale. The marble was carved by a contemporary of Andrea Mantegna, Antonio Lombardo, and was unpublished and unknown. No one knows how or when the sculpture arrived in England; it had possibly been purchased by an Englishman on the Grand Tour with an eye for quality. The vendors certainly had no idea as to its importance as it had been stored in a barn. Our research revealed that the marble *Dido of Carthage* had originally belonged to Alfonso I d'Este, 3rd Duke of Ferrara, and was one of a series of marbles carved by Lombardo and his workshop to decorate two rooms that formed a passage between the Palace and Castle at Ferrara. Other marbles from the set are divided between the Hermitage Museum, St Petersburg and the Louvre. Under the glare of numerous television cameras the Dido relief was purchased by us at the sale and later sold to Mrs Barbara Johnson, but not before a temporary export licence stop was imposed upon it.

Agnew's have also been involved in assisting museums to add to their collections and for some years now the National Gallery of Scotland in Edinburgh has been building up an impressive group of commemorative Renaissance and Baroque medals that is displayed alongside the paintings, furniture and sculpture. Not to be confused with military decorations, these double-sided bronze plaques were highly popular in the Renaissance and now form part of every major museum's holdings of decorative arts and sculpture. In the summer of 1990 we sold to the National Gallery of Scotland a superb bronze medal of the Ottoman Sultan Mohammed II (Plates 165a and 165b) by the Florentine sculptor Bertoldo di Giovanni. We know through Vasari's description of him that he was the pupil of Donatello and the teacher of Michelangelo; he thus links the greatest Florentine sculptors of the 15th and 16th centuries. His portrait was painted by Botticelli in his celebrated picture, *Young Man with a Medal*, in the Uffizi, so we also know what he looked like. Our example was, like the *Dido of Carthage* relief, unknown and unpublished, and is now on public display in Edinburgh.

No visitor to the Frick Collection in New York, the Wallace Collection in London or Waddesdon Manor in Buckinghamshire can fail to notice the superb French Renaissance enamels on display. These in general date from the late 15th to late 17th centuries and were collected and widely admired during the 19th and early 20th centuries. But during the period from the end of the War to the mid-70s, Limoges enamels were out of fashion and could be purchased for a fraction of their former value. It is mostly due to purchasing decisions of continental and American museums supported by discerning private collectors in France and Belgium that these enamels, are being bought once more. The British Rail Pension Fund also purchased Limoges enamels, setting new price levels when they bought a set of 12 plaques from Christie's in 1978 which had belonged to a client of ours, Arthur A. Houghton Jnr., who was well known for his collection of books and Persian miniatures. Arthur Houghton also possessed a large triptych of the *Annunciation and Nativity* (Plate 166) by a Limoges enameller called the Master of the Large Foreheads. Our research revealed that this triptych had once belonged to the Royal Prussian collections, and then the Kunstgewerbemuseum in Berlin before being sold by the Germans in the '20s. We were especially pleased, in 1983, to assist in the return of the triptych to its rightful home, by

Plate 164

ANTONIO LOMBARDO

c.1458-1516

Dido of Carthage

Marble, 19¾ x 10½ inches (52 x 27 cm.)

Barbara Piasecka Johnson collection, Princeton, 1988

(In association with Daniel Katz)

Plates 165a and 165b

GIOVANNI DI BERTOLDO

c.1420-1491

Sultan Mohammed II

Bronze, 3¾ inches (9.4 cm.)

National Galleries of Scotland, 1991

Plate 166

THE MASTER OF THE LARGE FOREHEADS

fl. 1500-1525

The Annunciation and Nativity

Enamel on copper, Nativity plaque, 8¼ x 6¾ inches (21 x 17.3 cm.)

Annunciation plaques, each, 8¼ x 2¾ inches (21.2 x 7.2 cm.)

Limoges, Musée Municipal de l'Evêché, 1981

selling it to the Musée de l'Evêché in Limoges.

One of the most important exhibitions of sculpture held in the last 20 years was that devoted to Giambologna and organised by the Victoria and Albert Museum in 1978. The aim of the exhibition was both to show that Giambologna was one of the most inventive of sculptors, and also to attempt to distinguish work by his own hand from that of his workshop. This resulted in a complete reappraisal of the bronzes by Giambologna and his circle. Whereas autograph works by Giambologna and his entourage were selling for tens of thousands of pounds at, for example, the Mentmore sale in 1978, by December 1989 a superb bronze of *The Dancing Faun* by a Netherlandish follower of Giambologna, Adriaen de Vries, sold for £6,820,000 at Sotheby's in London. The two bronzes that we have handled that are especially noteworthy in this context are *Hercules killing the Dragon Ladon* (Plate 167) by Felice Palma and *Rogero and Angelica* (Plate 168) by Ferdinando Tacca. The former shows the influence and style of Palma's master, Tiziano Aspetti, in its modelling, while adapting one of Giambologna's compositions from the *Twelve Labours of Hercules*. The *Rogero and Angelica* by Ferdinando Tacca is a discovery made by Agnew's in France. The composition was known through another example in the Louvre prior to the appearance of our bronze, but ours differed from it in that Tacca added decorative chasing to Rogero's helmet and treated the base in a different way. This bronze is acknowledged to be the finest of Ferdinando's subjects. Ferdinando Tacca's father, Pietro, was Giambologna's follower and principal assistant, and both father and son worked in the Borgo Pinti workshop in Florence, thus establishing a clear link between Tacca's work and that of the great Mannerist sculptor.

The market in bronzes of this date saw the dispersal of several collections in London, like the Robert Strauss collection in 1976, the Baron Hatvany collection in 1983, both sold at Christie's, and the Mentmore sale of 1977, sold by Sotheby's. While Algardi was one of the greatest exponents of Baroque sculpture in Rome besides Bernini, Foggini holds that honour in Florence, alongside his Tuscan contemporary Massimiliano Soldani-Benzi. The bronze purchased by us in 1983 of the *Suicide of Ajax* (Plate 162) by Foggini is notable because of its rarity, there being only two other examples: a bronze in the Art Gallery of Ontario, Toronto and a wax in the Doccia Museum in Sesto Fiorentino, Italy.

In the last few years we have handled two major works by Alessandro Algardi. The first, his marble portrait bust of *Antonio Cerri* (Plate 162), was one of the finest Algardis left in private hands to come on to the market in recent times. The second, a bronze sculpture of the *Virgin and Child* (Plate 169), was purchased by us at auction in New York in 1989. It was sold by the estate of Walter Chrysler Jnr., heir to the Chrysler automobile fortune. The sculpture had been on view at the Chrysler Museum in Norfolk, Virginia since 1979. The bronze was brought back to London where delicate cleaning revealed exquisite surface details which had hitherto been obscured, and it was purchased by an American private collector in 1990.

In the field of French 18th century sculpture we have handled three exceptional works: the earliest, a bronze of *Aria and Paetus* (Plate 171), is by Laurent Hubert and dates to around 1753. Research has revealed that the Parisian sculptor exhibited this bronze at the academy of Saint-Luc in the same year. We purchased the bronze, catalogued as 'Italian or French late 17th century', at the sale of Major-General Sir George Burns. *Aria and Paetus* was sold by us in February 1984 to a private collector who has recently displayed it at the Museum of Fine Arts, Boston. The second important 18th century sculpture is the *Bust of a Young Girl* (Plate

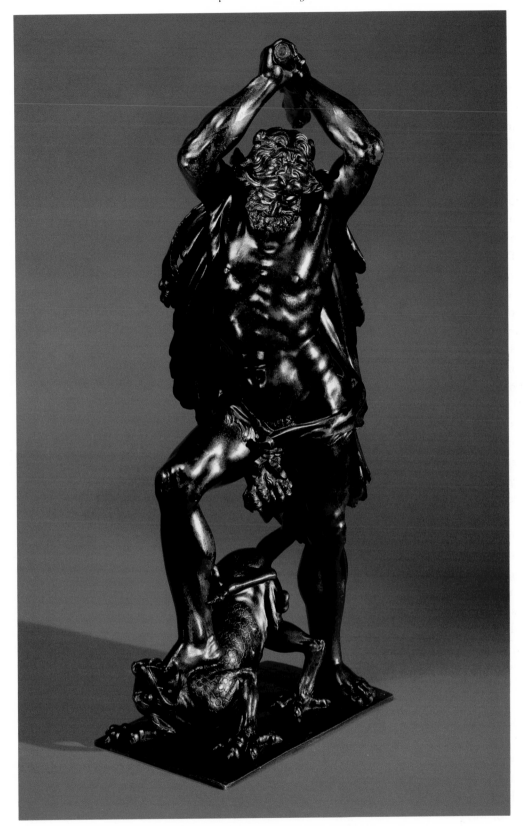

Plate 167

FELICE PALMA

1583-1625

Hercules and the Dragon Ladon

Bronze, 16⁷/₈ inches (43 cm.) high

Private collection, New York, 1987

Plate 168
FERDINANDO TACCA
1619-1686
Rogero and Angelica
Bronze, 16⁷⁄₈ inches (43.2 cm.) high
Private collection, New York, 1988

Plate 169

ALESSANDRO ALGARDI

1598-1654

Virgin and Child

Bronze, 19 inches (48.3 cm.) high

Private collection, New York, 1990

Plate 170

GIOVANNI BATTISTA FOGGINI

1652-1725

Cato (or Ajax) committing suicide

Bronze, 18¼ inches (46.6 cm.) high

The Metropolitan Museum of Art

1987 (1987.13)

Plate 171

LAURENT HUBERT

c.1725-1786

Aria and Paetus

Bronze, 20¾ inches (53 cm.) high

Private collection, 1984

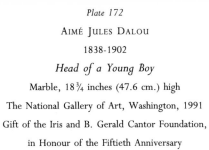

Plate 172

AIMÉ JULES DALOU

1838-1902

Head of a Young Boy

Marble, 18¾ inches (47.6 cm.) high

The National Gallery of Art, Washington, 1991

Gift of the Iris and B. Gerald Cantor Foundation,

in Honour of the Fiftieth Anniversary

Plate 173

JEAN-BAPTISTE LEMOYNE

1714-1778

Bust of a Young Girl

Marble, 12¼ inches (32.5 cm.) high

Tokyo Fuji Art Museum

173) by Jean-Baptiste Lemoyne sold to the Tokyo Fuji Art Museum and representing our first major sale of sculpture to a Japanese institution. The sculpture pre-dates the celebrated portraits of children by Jean-Antoine Houdon by some 40 years. The third, a marble of Mercury and Argus by Pierre-Etienne Monnot, we sold to the Toledo Museum of Art in 1992.

The exhibition *Romantics to Rodin*, organised by the Los Angeles County Museum of Art in 1978, focussed attention on French sculpture of the 19th century. We have dealt actively in this field over the last decade as 19th century sculpture is still very reasonably priced compared to earlier work, and enables buyers to acquire works of art of good quality with a modest budget. Among the many sculptures by Aimé Jules Dalou that we have bought and sold, the marble portrait *Bust of a Young Boy* (Plate 172) is most noteworthy. This long-neglected contemporary of Rodin excelled at portraits of children, and our portrait is the first in marble by

Plate 174

FRÉDÉRIC-AUGUSTE BARTHOLDI

1834-1904

Allegory of Africa

Bronze, 20 x 12½ inches (52 x 31.8 cm.)

National Gallery of Art, Washington, 1991

Gift of the 50th Anniversary Gift Committee

Dalou to enter the collection of the National Gallery of Art, Washington. The same museum purchased the *Allegory Of Africa* (Plate 174) by Frédéric-Auguste Bartholdi in 1991 as part of their 50th Anniversary celebrations. Best known for his colossal statue *Liberty Enlightening the World* (or the 'Statue of Liberty'), this is the first work by Bartholdi to enter the National Gallery's collection.

20th century sculpture is represented by the

Plate 175

FRANK DOBSON

1883-1963

Reclining Woman

Terracotta, 16 inches (41.7 cm.) long

Art Gallery of Ontario, Toronto, 1990

fine terracotta of a *Reclining Woman* (Plate 175) by Frank Dobson, purchased by the Art Gallery of Ontario. This terracotta, which dates from the early 1930s, shows the artist's skill in han-dling this medium and also illustrates Dobson's fascination with contemporary French sculpture.

WILLIAM AGNEW

Chapter 14

THE CORNING EWER

OF ALL THE WORKS OF ART ILLUSTRATED in this volume, one of the earliest, rarest and smallest is the 6¼ inch high glass ewer now in the Corning Museum of Glass. While we do not regularly deal in glass, we do act for clients on a commission basis advising on and selling works of art as diverse as musical manuscripts and furniture. The chief curator of the Corning Museum of Glass, David Whitehouse, has kindly provided the following description of this remarkable work of art.

'The Corning Ewer is the finest known example of Islamic cameo glass. The eggshell-thin body was blown from a gather of colourless glass that had been dipped in a pot of molten green glass to make the overlay. After it had been annealed, the ewer was cut, ground and polished by a master craftsman, who removed most of the overlay, creating a green design that stands in relief on a colourless background.

The principal decoration consists of a panel containing two almost identical scenes, one on each side of the body. Each scene contains a bird of prey standing on the rump of a horned animal and pecking at the back of its neck. The animal stumbles and turns to look at its adversary. Behind them, perched on a branch, is another bird. The creator of the ewer invested the scenes with a powerful sense of drama. At the same time, he enlivened the figures with unexpected touches. The hind legs of the animals and the wing coverts of the birds of prey, for example, terminate in half-palmettes.

The Corning Ewer is said to have been discovered in Iran, the reputed source of many other outstanding specimens of Islamic relief-cut glass. Indeed, the quantity of relief-cut glass coming from Iran is so great that scholars believe that much of it was made there.

The Corning Ewer, however, closely resembles a group of six rock crystal ewers that are attributed to workshops in Fatimid Cairo. One, in the Victoria and Albert Museum, is decorated with animals and birds of prey that resemble the animals and birds on the Corning Ewer. Another bears an Arabic inscription invoking 'the blessing of God on the Imam al-Aziz bi'llah'. Al-Aziz was the fifth Fatimid caliph, who reigned in Cairo from 975 to 996. A third rock crystal ewer has an inscription that refers to a Fatimid official in the years 1000-1008.

The strong similarity between the Corning Ewer and the rock crystal ewers suggests that they were all made at about the same time: the late 10th and early 11th centuries. It also suggests that they may have been made in the same place, and at present opinion is divided on where the Corning Ewer was made: in Egypt, like the rock crystal ewers, or in Iran, like so much of the finest Islamic relief-cut glass?

Regardless of its place of manufacture, the Corning Ewer is a masterpiece of glasscutting, and we count it among the greatest treasures of The Corning Museum of Glass.'

WILLIAM AGNEW

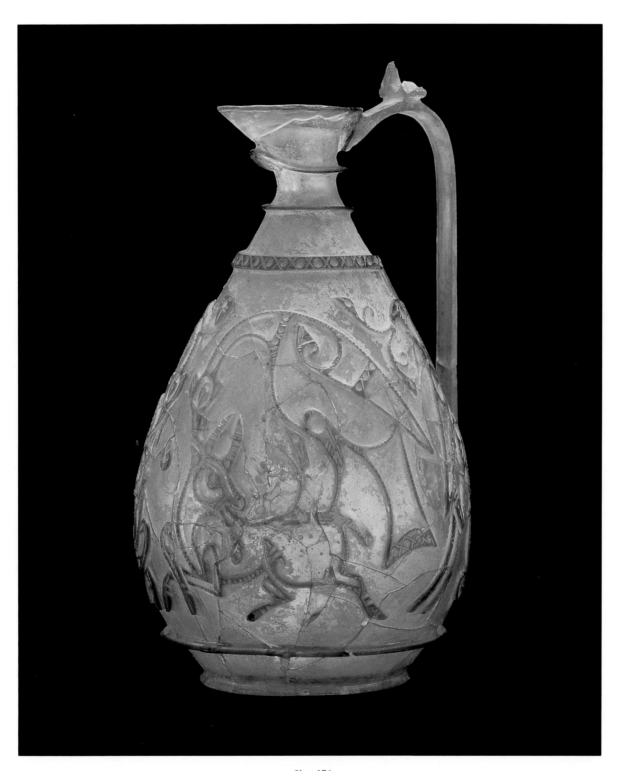

Plate 176

The Corning Ewer

Islamic, Egyptian or Iranian, about A.D. 1 000

Height 6¼ inches (16 c.m.) high

Clara S. Peck Endowment, The Corning Museum of Glass, 1985

Chapter 15

PRINTS

THE DECADE SURVEYED IN THIS BOOK was a busy one for the Print Department, involving the expansion of our activities and a change of emphasis in our stock. The arrival of Christopher Drake, at the beginning of 1988, to join the firm as director in charge of the Print Department provided the opportunity to build up the stock in 19th century French prints, in which he had previously specialised.

Master Print exhibitions were held in 1984, 1986 and 1989, each showing varied groups of interesting early prints. The 1989 Old & Modern Master Print catalogue, the first under Christopher's direction, included a representative selection of prints from Mantegna to Picasso. The finest Old Masters of this catalogue included Mantegna's *Madonna and Child* (Plate 177) , Dürer's woodcut of *The Four Riders of the Apocalypse* (Plate 178), and a superb complete set of Hendrik Goudt's seven engravings after works by Adam Elsheimer (Plate 179), all outstandingly rich impressions, with dazzling contrasts. The modern prints in the catalogue featured a superb impression of Toulouse-Lautrec's first lithograph, *The Englishman at the Moulin Rouge* (Plate 180). This was one of the rare impressions with the Englishman printed in grey rather than the usual dark red, which produces a very different effect. The subject was William Tom Warrener, an English painter who had studied at the Académie Julian. In 1892 (the year Lautrec made this print) Warrener moved into Lautrec's neighbourhood, Montmartre, to a house lived in by two more English artists, Charles Conder and William Rothenstein. In total contrast to the nightlife of the

Moulin Rouge, is Edvard Munch's night piece *Mondschein*, a luminous woodcut in five colours printed on tissue Japan paper (Plate 182). The impression which we exhibited of Matisse's *Grande Odalisque à la Culotte Bayadère* (Plate 183) was originally purchased from him by an American artist studying in Paris, Leon Kroll. In his memoirs Kroll recalls spending an afternoon with Matisse whilst he was working on the stone of the Odalisque, and encountering some difficulties: "You know, I can't get a firm line on this stone. It's terrible". But Kroll was able to offer the solution, "Well, the thing for you to do is to have it ground to a smoother surface. Your stone is too rough." Apparently the advice was effective. The final 'Modern Master Print' of the catalogue was Picasso's *Minotaure caressant une dormeuse* (Plate 184). This was one of only three impressions printed on parchment, which produced a particularly brilliant impression as the ink sits on the surface; in the standard edition on paper the ink is absorbed to some extent.

Whistler's etchings and lithographs have continued to be admired and enthusiastically collected. 1984 was the 150th anniversary of his birth, and there were celebratory exhibitions in London and especially in America. We were fortunate to have two large collections of his etchings to dispose of at that time, which contained a number of his most famous plates (Plate 186).

Over the decade we have handled a number of very fine Italian Old Master prints, including complete sets of Piranesi's *Carceri* and *Grotteschi* (Plate 187); and fine groups by Tiepolo and Canaletto. The *Imaginary view of Venice* (Plate

Plate 177

ANDREA MANTEGNA

c. 1431-1506

Madonna and Child known as *The Virgin of Humility*

Engraving, 8⁹/₁₀ x 9¼ inches (22.5 x 23.5 cm.)

Bartsch 8. Kristeller 3 p.445, second state with the halo

The Phillips Family collection, 1989

Plate 178

ALBRECHT DÜRER

1471-1528

The Four Riders of the Apocalypse

Woodcut, c.1497. 15¼ x 11 inches (38.9 x 28 cm.)

Bartsch 64; Hollstein, Meder 167 A

Private collection, USA, 1991

Plate 179

HENDRIK GOUDT

c.1585–c.1630

Ceres seeking her Daughter (after Adam Elsheimer)

Engraving, 11⁷⁄₈ x 9½ inches (32 x 24.7 cm.) Hollstein 5, only state

Art Gallery of Ontario, Toronto, 1991. Gift of the estate of Esther Gelber.

Plate 180

HENRI DE TOULOUSE-LAUTREC

1864-1901

L'Anglais au Moulin Rouge

Lithograph in colour. 15¾ x 20¹¹⁄₁₆ inches (40 x 52.5 cm.)

Delteil 12; Adriani 4 I; Wittrock 21

Private collection, USA, 1989

[200]

Plate 181

HENRI DE TOULOUSE-LAUTREC

1864-1901

La Femme au Tub

Lithograph in colour. 1896

15¾ x 20¹¹⁄₁₆ (40 x 52.5 cm.)

Delteil 183; Adriani 181 II; Wittrock 159

As published in the set Elles

Private collection, 1990

Plate 182

EDVARD MUNCH

1863-1944

Mondschein

Woodcut in colour, 1896

15¾ x 18½ inches (40 x 47 cm.)

Schiefler 81 A

Private collection, USA, 1989

12/50 Henri-Matisse

Plate 183

HENRI MATISSE

1869-1954

Grande Odalisque à la Culotte Bayadère

Lithograph, 1925   21¼ x 17¼ inches (54.2 x 44.2 cm.)

Duthuit 455. Signed in pencil and numbered 12 from the edition of 50. Private collection, UK, 1989

3/3

Plate 184

PABLO PICASSO

1881-1973

Minotaure caressant une Dormeuse

Drypoint. 1933. On parchment

11½ x 14⅛ inches (29.2 x 35.9 cm.)

Bloch 201; Geiser 369 iv/iv

Signed and numbered 3/3 in red ink.

3 impressions were printed on parchment, aside from the edition of 300 on Montval

Collection of Alan Cristea, 1989

Plate 185 (below)

PIERRE AUGUSTE RENOIR

1841-1919

La Danse à la Campagne (Premier planche)

Softground etching. c.1890

8¾ x 5½ inches (22 x 14.1 cm.)

Delteil 1

Private collection, 1989

Plate 186 (above)

JAMES ABBOTT MCNEILL WHISTLER

1834-1903

Nocturne: Palaces

Etching, 11⅝ x 7⅞ inches (29.5 x 19.8 cm.)

Kennedy 202 vii/ix

Art Gallery of Ontario, Toronto, 1982. Gift of Arthur and Ernest Gelber.

Plate 187

GIOVANNI BATTISTA PIRANESI

1720 - 1778

The Triumphal Arch

Etching and engraving and drypoint,

15½ x 21¾ (39.4 x 55.3 cm.)

From the complete set of 4 Grotteschi 1747-48

Robison 21-24, second edition, first issue (1750-c.1759)

James J. Stafford, 1991

Plate 188

GIOVANNI ANTONIO CANAL CALLED CANALETTO

1697-1768

Imaginary view of Venice

Engraving, $11^7/_8$ x $9^1/_2$ inches (32 x 24.7 cm.)

Bromberg 12, the undivided plate, only state before division.

The Toledo Museum of Art, 1983. Purchased with funds from the

Libbey Endowment, Gift of Edward Drummond Libbey.

188) was an exceptionally rare impression taken from the plate as Canaletto first completed it, before the plate was cut, for reasons unknown, making two separate prints. Dr. Ruth Bromberg in her *catalogue raisonné* recorded only six impressions, to which can be added this seventh print.

Although the vast majority of the prints we handle are acquired from private sources or dealers, we did of course participate in the two most important print auctions of the decade, the dispersal of some of the finest prints from the library at Chatsworth in 1985, and that of the collection of Dr. Blum in New York in 1988 at which we purchased Schongauer's *Man of Sorrows* (Plate 189), which was the finest example from a notable group.

In 1989 we made an interesting discovery in acquiring a group of four plates and cover for Géricault's *Série Anglaise* (Plate 192). The plates were still stitched in the original paper folder, which was numbered '3'. This established that the set of 12 prints was originally issued in parts, of which this set would have been the third. Of the two known complete sets (one cited by Delteil and the other formerly in the Neuerburg collection) both bear the number '1' on the portfolio cover. It could therefore be assumed that when the set was issued complete one of the part covers was used as the binder for the set. The Print Club of Cleveland purchased this set to commemorate the Museum's 75th anniversary in 1991.

Since the firm acquired a base in New York visits there have greatly increased and we have taken an active part in the New York print market. We have also exhibited regularly at the Works on Paper Fair at the Armory, and in the autumn of 1991 we had a stand at the first fair of the International Fine Print Dealers' Association. The central feature of our stand was an eye-catching collection of five lithographs by Odilon Redon. The print which excited the most interest was *Le Liseur* (Plate 190). The fast footwork of Mr Cliff Ackley of the Boston Museum of Fine Arts beat two private collectors to the front of the queue to reserve it. Not only was *Le Liseur* an extremely rare proof in the first state before letters, but it was inscribed by Redon (in decadent green chalk) to his friend J.K. Huysmans, author of the ultimate symbolist novel *A Rebours*. It was Huysmans who was largely responsible for publicising Redon's work through a passage in *A Rebours* where he describes a room in the house of his hero, Des Esseintes, furnished with Redon's pictures:

'productions of inconceivable eccentricity... These drawings passed all bounds, transgressing in a thousand ways the established laws of pictorial art, utterly fantastic and revolutionary, the work of a mad and morbid genius'.

Furthermore, the subject had personal significance to Redon, being a portrait of his friend and mentor Rodolphe Bresdin, who had taught him the technique of lithography. As a further act of homage the composition obviously refers to Rembrandt's etching of *St. Jerome in a dark chamber*.

Back at home we have been regular exhibitors at the London Print Fair, and one of our most interesting displays there was in 1991 when we devoted the stand to Théodore Roussel, a French artist who took the unusual step of coming to England at a time when most painters were travelling in the opposite direction. He settled in Chelsea and became a member of Whistler's circle; indeed it was Whistler who encouraged him to take up etching. Whistler's influence is apparent in Roussel's views of Chelsea and Fulham which he trims to the platemark leaving a tab for the signature in Whistler's fashion. However Roussel developed a unique contribution to the history of print-making. Perhaps because of his French background, he developed an interest in colour printing, and formulated the concept of the

Plate 189

MARTIN SCHONGAUER

first recorded 1465-c.1491

The Man of Sorrows

Engraving on copper, 8¾ x 6⅜ inches (22.3 x 16.4 cm.)

Bartsch 69 i/ii

Private collection, USA, 1989

Plate 190

ODILON REDON

1840-1916

Le Liseur

Lithograph. 1892

12³⁄₁₀ x 9³⁄₄ inches (31.3 x 23.8 cm.)

Mellerio 119; Gott 21 i/ii

Signed and dedicated in green chalk to J.K. Huysmans

Museum of Fine Arts, Boston, 1991. Gift of Katherine E. Bullard, in memory of Francis Bullard.

Plate 191 (above)

AUGUSTE RODIN

1840-1917

Henri Becque

Drypoint, pen and ink, 1885

8 x 6¼ inches (20.4 x 15.9 cm.)

Delteil 9, proof before Delteil's first recorded state

Musée Rodin, Paris, 1991 (Inv.G.7751)

Acquired with the assistance of the Societé Rodin

Plate 192 (below)

THÉODORE GÉRICAULT

1791-1824

Entrance to the Adelphi Wharf

Lithograph. 1821. 12¼ x 10 inches (31 x 25.5 cm.)

Delteil 40 ii/ii; Clement 31

The Cleveland Museum of Art, 1990

75th Anniversary gift of the Print Club of Cleveland

(CMA 90.51)

ENTRANCE TO THE ADELPHI WHARF.

London, Published by Rodwell & Martin New Bond Street. May 1821.

print, mount and frame as a complete decorative object. Where Whistler had experimented by painting frames to surround his oil paintings, Roussel printed his mounts and frames, and is the only artist known to have done so (Plate 193). He propounded his theory when he first exhibited the framed prints at the Goupil Gallery in 1899:

> 'It will be noticed that the mount on which each proof is laid is itself an etching printed in colours, as is also the frame surrounding the mount. I have adopted this arrangement in order that the central proof should, at least according to my ideas, form with its mount and frame, always specially printed for it, a complete harmony of colour, each proof so presented, being the result sometimes of as many as twenty four or even a greater number of printings'.

We were fortunate to acquire the only known complete set of his nine colour prints and frames (probably the original set exhibited at the Goupil Gallery), and they could not have found a more fitting home than the Victoria and Albert Museum.

Another occasion when a print went to a particularly appropriate home was the sale of a drypoint by Rodin of the writer Henri Becque to the Rodin Museum in Paris (Plate 191). This impression was a very rich progress proof with extensive work in pen and ink to indicate where further cross-hatching should be added to the plate. The proof came from the collection of the artist Jean-François Raffaelli, who was a friend of both Rodin and Becque throughout the 1880s. In 1886 Raffaelli wrote and illustrated an article defending the naturalism of Becque's plays, and in 1888 provided drawings for his 'Sonnets', so it is possible that this impression was a gift from Becque to Raffaelli.

We have put on several single-artist exhibitions in recent years including the prints of John Copley, organised in association with Gordon Cooke; and the etchings of Claude Gellée (le Lorrain). This latter coincided with the publication of Lino Mannocci's *catalogue raisonné*, and included impressions of all Claude's subjects except for the most extreme rarities.

Our most ambitious exhibition to date was that of the prints published by the Parisian dealer Ambroise Vollard from 1895-1913. This covered the most dynamic years of printmaking in the 19th century. Vollard had the courage and foresight to commission works from young and relatively unknown artists such as the Nabis: Bonnard, Vuillard and Ker-Xavier Roussel, and it was he who gave both Cézanne and Picasso their first one-man exhibitions. We mounted the exhibition in conjunction with Arcadia, in Tokyo, and showed it at the Ginza Art Museum in the summer of 1991, and then at Agnew's in London.

To accompany it we produced a lavish catalogue (in English and Japanese), the design based on Vollard's own publications. It is hoped that it will become a useful reference work as it illustrates a number of prints not illustrated elsewhere, notably those by Maurice Denis (Plate 195).

Vollard started by publishing mixed albums of prints by a surprising variety of artists, from Cézanne and Toulouse-Lautrec, to the lesser-known Scottish painter James Pitcairn-Knowles and the Hungarian Joszef Rippl-Ronai, all working in Paris at the time. This led on to albums by individual artists: Redon's *Temptation of St. Anthony*; Bonnard's *Quelques Aspects de la Vie de Paris*; Vuillard's *Paysages et Intérieurs* (Plate 196), and K-X Roussel's *Album de Paysages*. The final item of the catalogue was Picasso's *Suite de Saltimbanques* which marked the end of the first phase of Vollard's publishing career. The Saltimbanques (Plate 197) were the first prints Picasso made, executed in 1904-5. However, he only ever printed a handful of impressions, and sold the plates to Vollard, who had them steel-faced and then printed them in 1913 in editions of 250 on Van Gelder paper and either

Plate 193

THÉODORE ROUSSEL

1847-1926

Chelsea Palaces

Etching and aquatint in colour

$3\frac{1}{2}$ x $5\frac{1}{8}$ inches (8.8 x 13 cm.)

In original mount and frame designed and printed by the artist 1890-97

$18\frac{5}{8}$ x $19\frac{5}{8}$ inches (47.3 x 49.8 cm.)

Housberg 144

Victoria and Albert Museum, 1991. Courtesy of the Board of Trustees.

Plate 194

PIERRE BONNARD

1867-1947

La Petite Blanchisseuse

Lithograph in colour. 1896

11½ x 7¾ inches (29 x 19 cm.)

Roger-Marx 42

Private collection, USA, 1989

[214]

Plate 195

MAURICE DENIS

1870-1943

Le Reflet dans la Fontaine

Lithograph in colour. 1897

15¾ x 10 (40 x 25.5 cm.) Cailler 100

Cecil Higgins Museum and Art Gallery, Bedford, 1991

Plate 196

EDOUARD VUILLARD

1868-1940

La Cuisinière

Lithograph in colour. 1899

14 x 10^7/$_8$ inches (35.5 x 27.5 cm.)

Roger-Marx 42. From the complete set of 12 lithographs

and cover Paysages et Interieurs. Published by Ambroise Vollard, 1899

27 or 29 on antique Japan paper. We held one of the rare sets on Japan paper.

And finally we come to a sad landmark in the Print Department's history: William Plomer (Bill to almost everyone, and Plum to most in the firm) had become an integral part of both the firm and the London print world. His knowledge of Whistler and English mezzotints in particular, as well as an inexhaustible patience with all kinds of enquiry, were an enduring asset to the firm for 38 years. In August 1990 he retired, but both in Europe and

Plate 197

PABLO PICASSO

1881-1973

Le Repas Frugal

Etching. 1904. 18¼ x 14⅞ (46.3 x 37.7 cm.) Bloch 1.

Private collection, Japan, 1992

the United States, as well as in the London gallery, clients warmly ask after him, and he still illuminates his subject from time to time as invited lecturer.

Looking to the future, it is envisaged that we will continue to deal in the greatest names both in Old Master and Modern art in an age when, in many cases, paintings by the same masters are realistically unavailable.

SUSIE WILLIAMS, CHRISTOPHER DRAKE,
BILL PLOMER

Chapter 16

20TH CENTURY BRITISH PAINTINGS AND DRAWINGS

THE MAJORITY OF LATE 19TH AND 20TH century paintings with which Agnew's have dealt over the last 10 years are British, and the following chapter illustrates and describes 14 paintings and two works on paper sold over the decade. The quality and traditional character of most of the works are exemplified by the first picture, chronologically speaking: W.R.Sickert's *Le Lion Comique,* (Plate 198) which was sold to a private collector in 1989. Sickert had had a brief but successful career as an actor himself, before going to the Slade in 1881. Between 1887, the date of this painting - Sickert's earliest known theatrical scene - and the end of the century he produced a masterly series of scenes drawn from music hall life. Degas' individual forays into the modern theatrical world were a key influence in this picture. Sickert met Degas early in his career and the latter's work continued to exert a huge impact throughout Sickert's life; the use of a low viewpoint and the *repoussoir* figure of the violinist link the two halves of the composition. The influence of Degas and Manet is apparent here for the picture's tonality is pitched in a much higher key than Sickert's later music-hall paintings.

Philip Wilson Steer's *The Beach at Etaples* (Plate 199), which was painted in the same year as *Le Lion Comique,* provides, as a study from nature, an interesting contrast. The influences

of Manet and of Whistler are strong but Steer's use of tonal values, his palette knife technique, and the adoption of a low horizon combine to produce a unique and spontaneous depiction of outdoor light. The first owner of this picture was James Christie, a fellow student of Steer's in Paris in the 1880s, and it now belongs to a private collector in England.

S.J.Peploe is one of the great quartet of Scottish colourists. *Paris-Plage Normandy* of c.1909 (Plate 200) illustrates well the development of this distinctive school, and shows how French Painting, and particularly that by Manet, influenced their formative work. Peploe first went to France in 1893 to study at the Académie Julian. Until 1910, he spent some time each summer sketching in France at Etaples and at Paris-Plage with his friend and fellow colourist J.D. Fergusson. He painted a number of small panels and canvases depicting life at Paris-Plage: groups of figures in summer clothes and sun-drenched streets in that particular constant light which characterises coastal resorts. These paintings represent a development of the earlier schemes of light and colour of the Impressionists, but, as Stanley Cursiter writes in his 1947 monograph on Peploe, 'the creamy pigments are richer than ever...He was now a complete master of his technique and in these small pictures he is in holiday mood.'

Henry Lamb's *Two Nudes* (Plate 201) was in

Plate 198

W.R.Sickert A.R.A.

1860-1942

Le Lion Comique

Oil on canvas, 20 x 12 inches (51 x 31 cm.)

Private collection, 1988

Plate 199

PHILIP WILSON STEER O.M.

1860-1942

The Beach at Etaples

Oil on canvas, 14½ x 21½ inches (36.8 x 54.6 cm.)

Private collection, 1983

Plate 200

S.J.PEPLOE

1871-1935

Paris-Plage, Normandy

Oil on canvas, 8½ x 10½ inches (22.6 x 26.7 cm.)

Private collection, 1986

the collection of one of the great Bloomsbury society hostesses: Lady Ottoline Morrell, with whom he had a passionate affair. From 1906 until the outbreak of the First World War Lamb was based in London, where he mixed in the Bloomsbury and Hampstead circles, only occasionally making visits home to paint his family and Manchester friends. Significant influences upon him were his introduction to the work of Picasso, and the first Post-Impressionist exhibition of 1910, organised by Roger Fry. Around this time Lady Ottoline purchased a number of pictures, including this one, direct from the artist. Painted in oil and tempera on canvas its subject is uncertain, though the figures and composition can be compared to Picasso, whose symbolistic Rose and Blue period work Lamb would have seen in either 1910 or 1911, possibly at Gertrude Stein's house in Paris. In 1956 the picture was exhibited at the Leicester Galleries' *Pictures from Garsington* exhibition, where it was bought by Lady Juliette Huxley. The picture was sold to a private collector in 1990.

Harold Gilman was initially a disciple of Sickert and a member of the Camden Town group (later evolving into the London Group). However, he was influenced by the first Post-Impressionist exhibition of 1910 and, after that date, moved away from the traditions of the Sickert school towards a more modernist stance. *Kirkegarten, (Church Street) Flekkefjord* (Plate 203) was painted during Gilman's second visit to Sweden and Norway in 1913, during which he painted a series of landscapes. This represented a departure from his earlier work, in which he did not often paint landscapes. This picture shows the deep impression that van Gogh made on Gilman, visible most obviously in the work of 1912/13, through the thickness of impasto (Sickert subsequently described Gilman and his associate, Ginner, as 'the thickest painters in London'). The picture has also

been praised for its evocation of northern sunlight and radiance of pure colour. Gilman's *Portrait in Profile; Mary L.* (Plate 202) of the following year, shows a completely different technique adopted for the painting of a portrait in the classical idiom, yet in a modern style. Mary L. herself sits in repose against a highly decorative and almost abstract background. The only suggestion of depth is provided by the chair-back and the hint of a table-top on the right. Gilman painted her thrice in 1914; apart from this profile portrait, there is a three-quarter length study of her sitting, entitled *The Coral Necklace*, in the Brighton Art Gallery. This late phase in Gilman's short career, characterised by increasing use of heavy rich impasto, is now known as the 'Mosaic' period and this portrait is one of the key works. In 1986 we sold it to a British private collector.

David Bomberg's *Study for the Mudbath* (recto, Plate 204) is the first gouache of an extended sequence of drawings, watercolours and gouaches carried out in 1914 as a preparation for the painting *The Mud Bath*, now in the Tate, which was the crucial image in Bomberg's exhibition at the Chenil gallery that year. The origin of the image was the scene in Schevzik's Vapour Baths in Brick Lane, Whitechapel. Richard Cork quotes Lilian Bomberg as saying: "He must have stood on the balcony above the bath and observed the figures in movement down below, surrounded by those bare tiled walls - it was the perfect subject for him." The figures assert themselves with great conviction, and the use of colour is bold and exhilarating. There was in actual fact no mud bath at Schevzik's, but one theory about the origin of the title is that, while alluding to the general filthiness of the setting, it refers to the purifying properties of the mud-pack treatment available there, which in turn, parallels Bomberg's attempts to purge art of its superfluities.

Mary Chamot in *Country Life* in June 1926

Plate 201

HENRY LAMB R.A.

1885-1960

Two Nudes

Oil and tempera on canvas, 26½ x 21 inches (67.3 x 53.3 cm.)

Private collection, UK, 1990

(In association with Jonathan Clark Ltd.)

Plate 202

HAROLD GILMAN

1876-1919

Portrait in Profile; Mary L.

Oil on canvas, 24 x 20 inches (60 x 50 cm.)

Private collection, 1986

Plate 203

HAROLD GILMAN

1876-1919

Kirkegarten, Flekkefjord

Oil on canvas, 19⅓ x 24 inches (50 x 61 cm.)

Private collection, UK, 1985

Plate 204

DAVID BOMBERG

1890-1957

Study for the Mud bath I

Gouache on paper, 21 x 28 inches (53.5 x 71 cm.)

Private collection, 1990

(In association with Bernard Jacobson Ltd.)

describes Gwen John's *The Precious Book* (Plate 209) as 'unsurpassed for tenderness and beauty'. It is one of ten closely related paintings from a series all depicting the same model, known as 'The Convalescent'. She provided a perfect subject for Gwen John, who is renowned for her studies of introspection and meditation. All ten of this series, the largest known in her *oeuvre*, were painted between c.1916 and 1926 at 29 rue Terre Neuve in Meudon, near Paris - the chair in the picture appears in many other pictures, and the grey, chalky wall is that of her mansard studio room. Though associated with her brother, Augustus, and the bustling London artistic life he epitomised, Gwen herself retreated to France for most of her working life and chose a ruthlessly independent and solitary path. She had a little financial support, mainly through purchases by John Quinn, the American lawyer, who was one of the few collectors to give her recognition during her life-time, a recognition that has been bestowed so markedly since her death. One of the other nine works of this series is in the Tate, whilst others are in the collections of the Fitzwilliam Museum, Cambridge, Manchester City Art Gallery and that of Mr and Mrs Paul Mellon, Virginia.

Lotte Laserstein's painting *The Roof Garden, Potsdam* of 1928 (Plate 206) is an example of a 20th century painting that Agnew's has sold that has very little to do with any British tradition. In association with the dealer Caroline Stroude, Agnew's mounted two exhibitions of her work in 1987 and 1990. This picture shows a group of friends, in front of a detailed depiction of the Potsdam skyline. The spire to the right of the girl in yellow is the Church of St.Nicholas and the dome to the right of the man seated on our side of the dining table is that of the New Palace. Laserstein is still alive, and now lives and paints in Sweden, having fled Germany, her birthplace, before the Second World War. Her great friend, Traute Rose, describes the creation of this work: "the very long canvas was first transported to Potsdam on the Berlin railway, and then by horse-drawn carriage to its destination with friends who had a roof garden overlooking Potsdam. The friends were roped in for the first sketch, taking their places to decide upon the poses. The figures were only sketched in, because the view of Potsdam had to be painted first. Then the picture had to be transported back to the new studio with high windows, so that Lotte had outdoor lighting like the roof garden. Then the long task began with the various models. My position on the outside left in front of the railing was decided upon, as well as my husband's position with his dog at his feet. The figure in the pullover in the middle of the picture was another girl at first, but she did not last out and was replaced by the girl in the yellow pullover. The romantic man sitting next to her also had an unsuitable predecessor, and much to his displeasure, he was wiped out. The girl in the green dress in the foreground was suitable, but she could not bear standing, so I stood in for the legs. (My husband) Ernst had the most difficult pose as it was hard to hold the position of the propped arm and the tilted head. The dog was replaced by a fur skin because he didn't like Ernst's feet. The models had their hearts and souls in the job because they knew that Lotte was creating a great work."

Cacti in Greenhouse, Cookham Dean (Plate 207) is by Sir Stanley Spencer, an artist whose international reputation now exceeds that of any figurative artist of the first half of the 20th century. By 1937 Spencer had returned to his beloved Cookham, the village in Berkshire on the banks of the Thames, where he had been born and brought up. The year from September 1937 was a fertile and productive period that resulted in 40 pictures that his dealers, Tooth's, were able to sell unusually quickly.

Plate 205

JOHN MINTON A.R.A.

1917-1957

A Street Corner in Jamaica

Oil on canvas, 30 x 25 inches (76.2 x 63.5 cm.)

The Yale Center for British Art, Paul Mellon Fund, 1985

Plate 206 (above)

LOTTE LASERSTEIN

b.1898

The Roof Garden, Potsdam

Oil on panel, 43¾ x 81 inches (111.1 x 205.7 cm)

Private collection, Scotland, 1990

Plate 207 (below)

SIR STANLEY SPENCER R.A.

1891-1959

Cacti in the Greenhouse at Cookham Dean

Oil on canvas, 20 x 30 inches (51 x 76 cm)

Private collection, 1986

Spencer painted flower studies at odd times in his life, doubtless deriving satisfaction from the texture and colour of vegetation; certainly this picture, painted in 1938 and very close in style to others of the same date such as *The Greenhouse* (formerly in the collection of Gerald Kelly), is a distillation of the passion and obsessive sensuality that permeates all his painting.

Largely self-taught, Keith Vaughan has become a pivotal figure in mainstream British painting. Through association with painters such as Minton, Ayrton and Sutherland, he became involved in the Neo-Romantic Movement, his landscapes providing settings for the human figure. *A Wold Farm* of 1945 (Plate 208) demonstrates the combination of his pessimistic feelings about the isolation of man, especially that experienced universally after a harrowing war, and an ability to convey the beauty of the landscape in which man finds himself. Many of his pictures reflect his homosexuality, but references to other aspects of his character are numerous: his later works included abstractions of landscape and fantasy paintings inspired by the poems of Rimbaud and Baudelaire. An Honorary Fellow of the Royal College of Art and a respected teacher, Vaughan continued to exhibit, despite terminal cancer, until the year of his suicide. His journals, which he started to keep in 1939, sensitively record his life and his career as a painter, and close with the overwhelmingly sad description of his taking of an overdose. Agnew's are responsible for the work remaining in his estate, which includes many working drawings. His complete journals, from 1939-77, amount to 62 notebooks and a selection, edited by Alan Ross, was published in 1989.

Landscape with Bottle Tree (Plate 211) of 1945 was sold, in 1984, to a private collector in Australia. By one of the foremost Australian painters of this century, Russell Drysdale, it has thus returned to its place of conception. Drysdale, unlike Sidney Nolan and his other contem-

poraries, was a countryman and approached his work with an awareness of the Australian interior that has always shaped his pictures. Though owing a debt to European Surrealism, *Landscape with Bottle Tree* confirms the vision of a wholly Australian outlook of observed reality. A tour of New South Wales in 1944 led to a series of paintings recording the effect of the drought that he witnessed there. This picture was exhibited at the Macquarie Galleries in Sydney in 1949 and then at the Leicester Galleries in London in the following year. His experiments with form are unique, and the success of his individual style is summed up well by Patrick McCaughey, who writes: 'Drysdale's curiosity about Surrealism took root in the Australian landscape and the paintings and drawings of the period have both the luminosity of the dream and the grit of reality.'

Birdman with Pots by Edward Burra (Plate 210) is now in the collection of the Hove Museum and Art Gallery in Sussex. It is the larger of two watercolours on this theme dating from 1947. Burra's extraordinary imagery does not allow him to be placed in a definable position in British art. He painted almost entirely in watercolour, the conventional British medium, but his work rejects any traditional legacies. His obsessive concentration on objects and their juxtapositions links him with Wadsworth, Hillier and other Surrealists, but his exotic colours and his ability to imbue figures with menace and enigma set him apart from other narrative artists. He wrote a letter which goes some way to explaining this picture: 'A Birdman, he was very eccentric and always dressed up in school boys knickers and a neat cap so he could shin up a palm to look at a vulture's egg.' (Letter to William Chappell, c.1945).

The Yale Center for British Art has, since 1985, been the owner of *A Street Corner in Jamaica* (Plate 205) which was painted just after Minton's return to London from the West

Plate 208

Keith Vaughan

1912-1977

A Wold Farm

Oil on canvas, 24 x 32 inches (61 x 81 cm.)

Private collection, Republic of Ireland, 1990

Indies in 1951. Minton, like his close friend Keith Vaughan, was a deeply emotional homosexual whose life has been extensively mythologised: on the one hand to create the image of a gay, carefree, Soho-Bohemian, and on the other to suggest an introspective, fragile and deeply dedicated artist who took his own life at the age of 39. At the time when this picture was completed, Minton had been teaching at the Royal College of Art, but had taken a sabbatical to escape the English winter. The showing of some of the resulting pictures prompted the critic John Berger to write: `One senses Jamaica as a definite place in these picture - the nights of unreal moonlight, the false animation of the people in the wooden cafés beneath Coca Cola advertisements and naked light bulbs. And at the same time one is aware of the painter's sympathy, of the validity of his human values.' (*Art News & Review*, 22 September 1951). Minton himself was profoundly moved by the dichotomy of the island's spirit: `Daily the planes take off, the ships call, the tourists arrive, spend their money and depart. And meanwhile beneath this surface life, the life of the island, the inner conflict of politics, race, wealth, poverty and unemployment made acute by the crumbling of colonial life which is forever past, goes on: for the island like everywhere else, faces the problem of its equilibrium in a mad world. And the visitor, unless he wishes to take sides, must leave: remembering in the icy January London snow, the kindness and hospitality, the warm golden days of the seashore, the strange haunting landscape and the island's sadness.' (*Vogue*, November 1951.)

Barbara Hepworth's *Quartet, Anthroplasty* (Plate 212) is a major work amongst the set of operating-theatre drawings which she executed between 1947 and 1949. During the illness of one of her daughters, who was in hospital in Exeter, Hepworth became the friend of a sur-

geon who suggested that she watch an operation, to extend the study she had undertaken of portraying people at work. Over two years she watched at orthopaedic hospitals in Exeter and in London: the drawings were all done immediately afterwards. Anthroplasty is the term applied to the operation for the making of a new joint. She describes the experience as follows: `...I expected that I should dislike it; but from the moment when I entered the operating theatre I became completely absorbed by two things: first, the extraordinary beauty of purpose and co-ordination between human beings all dedicated to the saving of life, and the way that unity of idea and purpose dictated a perfection of concentration, movement and gesture; and secondly by the way this special grace (grace of mind and body) induced a spontaneous space composition, an articulated and animated kind of abstract sculpture very close to what I had been seeking in my own work.'

In 1989 Agnew's sold a portrait to the only collection in the UK which can rival the Tate Gallery in its record for purchasing modern art, the Saatchi collection. *A Young Painter* (Plate 213) is by Lucian Freud, who has been acclaimed as the most penetrating portraitist at work today. The distinguishing feature of his work is that he consistently paints from life rather than adopting more sophisticated imagery, which is often perceived as the hallmark of modern artists. For Freud, this is an article of faith. He says of his work: `I would like my portraits to be of the people, not like them. Not having the look of the sitter, being them...As far as I am concerned, the paint is the person.' (Lawrence Gowing, *Lucian Freud*, London, 1982 pp.190-1.) This approach endows his work with an authority and a vitality which are at the heart of its enduring importance.

MAGDALEN EVANS

Plate 209

GWEN JOHN

1876-1939

The Precious Book

Oil on canvas laid down on panel, 10½ x 8¾ inches (27.7 x 22.3 cm.)

Private collection, 1988

Plate 210

EDWARD BURRA

1905-1976

Birdmen and Pots

Watercolour, 32½ x 22¾ inches (80 x 57.8 cm.)

The Hove Museum and Art Gallery; acquired with V & A Grant-in-aid

and assistance from the National Art Collections Fund, 1983

Plate 211

SIR RUSSELL DRYSDALE

1912-1981

Landscape with a Bottle Tree

Oil on canvas, 26 x 40 inches (66 x 101.6 cm.)

The Robert Holmes à Court collection, 1984

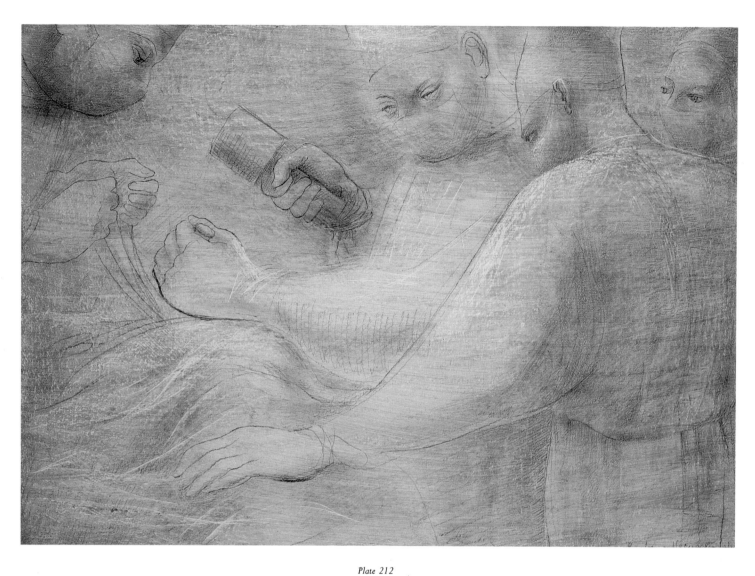

Plate 212

Barbara Hepworth

1903-1975

Quartet, (Anthroplasty)

Pencil and oil on panel, 9¾ x 12¾ inches (24.7 x 32.3 cm.)

Private collection, UK, 1985

Plate 213

LUCIAN FREUD

b.1922

Portrait of a Young Painter

Oil on canvas, 16 x 15 inches (40.6 x 38.1 cm.)

The Saatchi Collection, London, 1989

(In association with Bernard Jacobson Ltd.)

Chapter 17

A 20TH CENTURY CORPORATE COLLECTION: BARINGS

THE FIRM OF BARINGS HAVE A LONG tradition of collecting pictures and supporting contemporary painting: a tradition started in the 18th century and confirmed in 1806 by the commission from Lawrence of a portrait of their founder, Sir Francis Baring with his brother and son-in-law, both partners in the bank. Agnew's have had the great privilege of helping form some sections of their extensive collection, particularly in the field of early English watercolours and 20th century British painting.

Ten years ago a great impetus for an increasingly active acquisitions policy was provided by Baring Brothers' move to a new 20-storey building at No. 8 Bishopsgate. In 1989 Baring Asset Management moved up the road into part of a new spectacular office complex, the Broadgate development, above Liverpool Street railway station. As the nature of merchant banking has changed, so the demand for a greater number of small rooms has increased: thus, inadvertently, a much larger amount of wall space has been created by these changes. As many rooms in both buildings face out towards daylight, considerations of conservation require hanging oil paintings, rather than works on paper, on any wall that may be affected by direct sunlight.

There are now two distinct collections of 20th century pictures which Agnew's have helped to form: the first, housed at No.8 Bishopsgate, is distinguished by a variety of high quality, mostly figurative, paintings dating up to the mid-1950s, and the second, in the recently completed offices at No.155, is wholly contemporary in character.

One of the earliest pictures in the first, 'early modern' group is Philip Wilson Steer's *Ludlow Castle, Stormy Sky* of 1898 (Plate 214) which provides a good contrast to the majority of other pictures in the group which date from after the first War: some good examples being John Tunnard's *Red River* of 1945 (Plate 215), Leonard Rosoman's *The Burnt-Out Fire Appliance* of 1949 (Plate 216) and Michael Ayrton's *Vines before Easter* also of 1939-40 (Plate 217).

B.A.M. Ltd.'s collection has a very different character to that at No.8 Bishopsgate. The criteria dictating its formation are quite different, and the aim has been to create a collection of modestly priced work by contemporary British artists. Emma Sergeant's *Imran Khan* of 1986 (Plate 218) is a refreshing contrast to the average picture to be found at the end of a bank's corridor: it provides a good subject for conversation for visitors to the private rooms. Len Tabner's *Lindisfarne Castle with Bamburgh beyond, 11 am March 1987, Looking over by Emmanuel Head* (Plate 219) hangs in their foyer behind the reception desk and arrests one's attention on coming out of any one of eight lifts.

MAGDALEN EVANS

Plate 214

PHILIP WILSON STEER O.M.

1860-1942

Ludlow Castle, Stormy Sky

Oil on canvas, 20 x 26 inches (50.8 x 66 cm.)

1985

Plate 215

JOHN TUNNARD R.A.

1900-1971

Red River

Oil on board, 21¼ x 27½ inches (54 x 69.8 cm.)

1990

Plate 216

LEONARD ROSOMAN O.B.E. R.A.

b.1913

A Burnt out Fire Appliance

Oil on canvas, 29½ x 39½ inches (75 x 100.3 cm.)

1990

Plate 217

MICHAEL AYRTON

1921-1975

Vines before Easter

Oil on board, 23½ x 35⅜ inches (59 x 90 cm.)

1986

Plate 218

EMMA SERGEANT

b.1959

Portrait of Imran Khan

Oil on canvas, 86¼ x 27⅝ inches (219 x 70 cm.)

1989

Plate 219

LEN TABNER

b.1946

Lindisfarne Castle with Bamburgh beyond, 11 am,

Thursday, looking over by Emmanuel Head, March

Mixed media on heavy cotton paper, 109 x 200 inches (277 x 508 cm.)

1989

Chapter 18

GEOFFREY AGNEW

GEOFFREY AGNEW DIED ON 22 NOVEMBER, 1986. Still in harness at the age of 78, he had been in the firm for just over 55 years - almost a third of its existence. He was the author of the first volume of the firm's history, *Agnew's 1817 - 1967*, had been chairman throughout the period covered by the second volume, *A Dealer's Record 1967 - 1981*, and died almost midway through the years dealt with here. This memoir aims to give a short account of his career as a dealer and of the exceptional contribution he made to the firm.

Geoffrey joined the firm in the autumn of 1931 at the bottom of the slump. Agnew's was full of pictures bought in better times which had become quite unsaleable and the gallery was almost devoid of visitors. Geoffrey set about attracting new clients by arranging exhibitions of pictures and drawings at modest prices: Sickert, Duncan Grant and Vanessa Bell among living artists, and work by Derain, Pissarro, Degas and Cézanne. During this time he was a salesman on commission and when he became engaged to Doreen Jessel in 1934 he promised his future father-in-law that he would double his commission earnings each year; this he succeeded in doing until the outbreak of War in 1939.

Exempted from military service, Geoffrey spent the War as a master at Eton, a job he had been offered on leaving Cambridge. A strong pedagogic streak, no doubt always latent, blossomed at Eton and he proved to be a first-rate teacher, as I can testify from personal experience. His liking for a captive audience remained and he later enjoyed taking clients round exhibitions or museums where his booming voice often corralled other visitors into his audience.

At Eton, too, he made some useful future contacts, for among his pupils were Jo Floyd, later Chairman of Christie's, Michael Jaffé, who was to become Director of the Fitzwilliam Museum, and boys with distinguished picture collections in the family such as Johnny Althorp and Christopher Loyd. Others, like Patrick Plunket, were to make collections of their own.

Back at Agnew's after the War Geoffrey set about expanding the firm's business. In the Spring of 1947 he decided to revive contacts in America and accordingly set off there with Doreen together with Colin Agnew, who had run Agnew's New York branch in the 1920s. This was the first of over 100 Atlantic crossings that Geoffrey made but this trip did not go entirely to plan. Much ground was covered and at each new hotel Colin duly put his shoes outside his bedroom door expecting them to be cleaned, as would happen in England. Instead they were invariably stolen and it was not until this had recurred several times that Geoffrey managed to persuade Colin to desist.

Replacing the shoes ate up much of their meagre dollar allowance. And it was not until the very end of the trip that Geoffrey made his first sale on American soil. The picture, *Christ at the Column*, attributed - perhaps optimistically - to Castagno, was sold to a New York dealer. A triumphant cable to London received the reply that the picture had just been sold out of the Bond Street window a few hours previously. As the picture had been in stock for over 14 years this was cruel luck.

After the first visit, however, Geoffrey's

JOHN WARD R.A.
Sir Geoffrey Agnew. 1972

record in America and Canada was one of virtually unbroken success. He sold pictures to nearly every important collection of Old Masters, publicly and privately owned, in both countries. He always greatly enjoyed New York which he found particularly stimulating and it was there that he renewed his friendship with Rudolf Heinemann, whom he had met in Munich before the War. Over the next 20 years Rudolf and Agnew's did a great deal of shared business together, much of it very profitable.

Yet success in America in no way resulted in Geoffrey neglecting his clients in Britain. A glance through Agnew's correspondence files reveals how assiduous he was in keeping in touch with them and it is not surprising that many of them became close friends. He was also on very good terms with the staff of museums in this country, thus helping to break down the barrier of mistrust that used to exist between museums and the trade. Proof of his success can be seen in his being asked to bid at auction for the National Gallery on a number of occasions as well as for other U.K. museums.

In 1959 Paul Mellon began to collect English pictures on a prodigious scale (700 in one year alone, I have been reliably informed) and Geoffrey seized the opportunity to sell him literally scores of pictures and watercolours in the 1960s and '70s. Paul Mellon became not only Geoffrey's best client but the best client in the whole history of the firm. Geoffrey's early years in the firm had the result that he never lost his pleasure in selling minor pictures. I remember Basil Taylor, who helped Paul Mellon form his collection, telling me how amazed he was to find that Geoffrey took as much trouble in selling a £30 watercolour as he did over Constable's *Hadleigh Castle*. But taking trouble was in Geoffrey's nature and accounted in great measure for his success.

At times during this period of the '60s and '70s Geoffrey accounted for such a large proportion of Agnew's business that he tended to employ the first person singular when describing the firm's activities. This foible was recognised by his colleagues and by some of his clients although few of them were bold enough to tease him about it. However, when Geoffrey said one day "I bought a magnificent Canaletto last week," the Duke of Northumberland replied, deadpan, "Heavens, Geoffrey, you must be *fearfully* rich!"

Like many very busy people, Geoffrey was constantly being asked to take on other jobs outside Agnew's and, although they took up much precious time, he devoted to them the same energy and attention to detail as he did to the firm's affairs. His advice was always practical and cogently argued so that he was much in demand to serve on all sorts of committees connected with the arts. He rendered them yeoman service and was rewarded in 1973 with a Knighthood, an honour which gave him enormous pleasure.

Geoffrey was a dealer through and through and this coloured his whole attitude to works of art. In common with his mentor, Joe Duveen, he sometimes felt aggrieved at the number of pictures in museums and churches. I remember

going with him to the Badia in Florence, a church Geoffrey had not previously visited, to see the wonderful Filippino Lippi of *The Vision of Bernard*. After looking at it Geoffrey said wistfully, "My goodness, I'd like to have that in stock."

In his obituary notice of Geoffrey in *The Independent* Dick Kingzett drew attention to Geoffrey's gifts as a showman and those were certainly extraordinary. But his flair as a salesman was underpinned by more solid virtues including patience, perseverance and meticulous attention to detail. His skill as a negotiator was never shown to better advantage than in his dealings with the Liechtenstein Collection from which he succeeded in obtaining a superb group of pictures for the National Gallery of Canada after months of discussion, offer and counteroffer. Yet in the end it was his firm confidence in his own judgement, and his ability to impart this to his clients so that they felt entirely reassured when buying pictures from him, that was his greatest gift. It was this that made him preeminent in his profession and which, even in his final illness, which he faced with exemplary courage, he retained to the last. During his long career he had seen the firm to which he was so devoted go through some difficult times but, due mainly to his skill and leadership, he was able to leave it in excellent shape.

In 1977 Geoffrey sold the late Rembrandt portrait, *Man in a fur-lined Coat*, to the Toledo Museum, Ohio. At the time the retiring director of the museum, Otto Wittmann, whose reputation was second to none in his profession, wrote to Geoffrey confirming the purchase and referring to Geoffrey as, 'a great friend and the finest dealer I have ever known.' This is a verdict which Geoffrey's partners would certainly endorse while at the same time providing a tribute that would surely have pleased Geoffrey himself.

EVELYN JOLL

Chapter 19

SOME COLLECTORS
I REMEMBER

*'I look upon anecdotes as debts due to the public,
which every man when he has that kind of cash by
him, ought to pay.'*

5th Earl of Orrery, 1741

IN 1967 GEOFFREY AGNEW COMPLETED THE Herculean task of compiling the history of the first 150 years of the firm. His account of affairs up to the end of the second World War went into considerable detail and contained vivid portraits of the personalities involved. When he reached 1945 he felt that the time was too close to write much about our clients from then on, and confined himself to describing the more important events of the next 22 years. The introduction to the catalogue of the exhibition which we arranged in Geoffrey's memory in 1987 gave me the chance to recall some of the colleagues and clients with whom he had dealt. The danger inherent in this approach was that the result might read like a gossip column. I have nothing against gossip writers when they do it as well as Horace Walpole or Mr Creevey, but sadly most of them do not. However, some people seemed to enjoy reading it and two friends, whose judgement I value, sug-

MR JOHN PAUL GETTY
Courtesy of the Hulton Picture Company

gested that I should try to evoke a few others among the more idiosyncratic characters who visited us regularly in the two decades after the War.

I have chosen 11 men whose personalities will, I hope, interest other people as much as they have intrigued me. I do not think that I have fantasticated them, but time always supplies some element of fantasy. We should remember L.P.Hartley's, 'The past is a foreign country. They do things differently there.'

Despite, or perhaps because of, the disparity in their characters and backgrounds, Colin Agnew and Paul Getty became close friends. Their conversation had one interesting phonetic feature. Mr Getty, by omitting the letter 'i', reduced Colin's Christian name to a monosyllable, while Colin contrived to get three separate sounds into the name Paul, which he always spoke with a rising inflexion. Mr Getty bought Sutton Place in the 1960s, and this was the period when he most

SIR DAVID SCOTT

enjoyed acquiring pictures. The vast rooms of that great Tudor mansion allowed him to indulge his taste for really large canvases, and the full-length portraits by Gainsborough and Batoni, the enormous hunting scenes and game larders by Snyders, and a life-size nude by Palma Vecchio all looked wonderful in their new setting. At this date he rarely bought without consulting Colin, but as neither man had any real sense of time, their meetings required considerable stage-management. At a lunch party celebrating Colin's 90th birthday, Mr Getty arrived half an hour late with the ingenuous excuse that he had miscalculated how long it would take him to walk from the Ritz to

Boodles Club in St. James's Street.

Once, in Colin's absence, I showed him three pictures which he was considering - a portrait by Veronese, another by Tintoretto and the centre panel of an altarpiece by Girolamo di Benvenuto. Asking for the appropriate volumes of Bryan's *Dictionary of Painters*, so that he could study the entries for these artists, he read slowly through them marking the place he had reached in the text with his forefinger. Eventually, thunder rumbled in the distance, and he looked up and asked if it was gun-fire; when I said I thought not, he moved to the door saying "If Mr Colin recommends them, I'll take all three." Feeling that further conversation was needed, I asked what the roses were like at Sutton that summer. He said that they were "just fine", and taking out a notebook, made an entry. A year later, I received a letter inviting me to lunch so that I could come and see his garden. I am glad to have had the chance to record this act of kindness on the part of a man who is more often remembered as having installed a pay-phone for the use of his weekend guests.

David Scott started collecting Victorian pictures when they were entirely out of fashion. He did this, not looking for bargains, but because he really loved and understood them. He could draw on an enormous field at that date, but he had a sensitive eye and everything he chose was enchanting of its particular kind. Himself the least snobbish of men, he never bought a picture for the artist's name, but always because it said something special to him. His taste was not wholly old-fashioned as he admired and owned the work of contemporary artists like John Tunnard, and he seemed to treat all pictures with the same gentle courtesy that he extended to his many friends. A colleague described him as looking like an ambassador at the turn of the century, and the analogy was fair allowing for the fact that he always wore blue rubber-soled Dunlop Bungies, which in no way undermined his natural dignity. He enjoyed a long and successful career in the diplomatic service, but his other deep passion was gardening. A garden for him was a living thing, and just as he could never resist buying one more picture, so he was forever creating new borders and settings for the plants about which he knew so much.

My wife, when she first met David, was very worried about our dog who was suffering from some mysterious ailment and looked very sorry for himself. "You must remember," he assured her, "that dogs are natural ham actors." This diagnosis proved accurate, and it was typical of his very practical sympathy. Tradescant's 'Diary' in *The Garden* wrote of him, "His eye for quality in plants was as clear-sighted as his views of people. He loved both and was surrounded through his long life by the very best of both." For me he was Chaucer's 'very parfit gentil knight'.

The most loyal visitor to the private views of our Annual Watercolour Exhibitions was the Rev. E.P. Baker, the rector of a small parish in the depths of Oxfordshire. Although a member of another faith, his small, slightly portly figure and twinkling spectacles recalled Father Brown. He had, too, the rock-like character and physical courage of Chesterton's priest. Punctual arrival at the head of the queue which formed up by 9.15 on the January Monday morning meant for him rising in the small hours and manoeuvring a moped along frozen lanes to catch the milk train from Kingham to Paddington, but he never failed to appear. In the grim winter of 1963, snow drifts blocked his way to the station and, as often happened in that Siberian season, the train's heating system had broken down. His arrival in Bond Street with chips of frozen snow still clinging to his person recalled that epic picture of polar heroism, 'A Very Gallant Gentleman', in which Captain Oates stag-

THE REVEREND E.P. BAKER
Courtesy of the Oxfordshire Archives

gers out into the blizzard. The queue, with whom he was a great favourite, set to work to defrost his outer clothing while we from inside sent out a nip of something warming for the inner man. By common consent he was then allowed first choice in the Exhibition, and had soon made his annual purchase of two drawings, and returned to his normal rosy self.

He was a man who liked to overcome obstacles in pursuit of works of art. His must have been an unpleasant journey even when the January weather was mild, but he rejected offers to look at drawings in comfort at other times of the year. He seemed to find - and he was not alone in this - an extra dimension of pleasure in the competitive atmosphere of the queue. We met him in Warsaw, which we were visiting in the cushioned luxury of a package tour. Characteristically, he had made his own way across Northern Europe, although, I believe, not on his moped, since he was moving on to Prague on Polish State Railways. This much-loved man left his collection to be sold for the benefit of the Society of Antiquaries, to whom he was devoted.

Another of our clients who thought that the pleasure we derive from works of art increases in ratio to the difficulties we experience in arriving in front of them, was a Russian emigrant who had started his career in the Hermitage Museum. The fullest enjoyment of Giorgione's altarpiece could, he claimed, only be realised if we had walked from Venice to Castelfranco. Ephraim Shapiro worked in London in the Russian department of the B.B.C. Wartime conditions suited this complicated man, as he suffered from chronic insomnia and liked fire-watching by night while emerging in daylight to make predatory raids on the thinly-attended sale-rooms which provided a happy hunting ground for someone with eyes as sharp as his. His conversation had the inconsequence that Chekhov gave to his older characters and it was larded with Russian proverbs, many of which he was suspected of having invented himself. There was, however, nothing phony about his powers of connoisseurship, and looking at pictures with him was fascinating. Struwwelpeter hair streaming behind him, he took exhibitions at the run, a manic smile of glee overtaking his features when he spotted a wrong attribution. He had the Russian love of obfuscation, and indulged it to the full in his will, in which he left several pictures to the Hermitage. As he had become an English citizen and relations between ourselves and the Soviet Union were, when he died, a great deal pricklier than they are today, this caused considerable

MR EPHRAIM SHAPIRO

suspicion and distrust among the fiscal authorities of both countries. He would have relished the confusion which must have arisen.

A warning flashed across Europe in 1907 when Max Liebermann wrote from Amsterdam to Dr Bode in Berlin, "There is a redheaded young man here whom we must watch". This '*rotharriges Jungling*' was the 23-year-old Frits Lugt who was then working for the auctioneers Frederik Muller et Cie and the message led to an invitation to visit Dr Max Friedländer in that great training ground for art historians, the Print Room of the Kaiser Friedrich Museum. Lugt's arrival in Berlin coincided with that of Colin Agnew, whom we had sent to open a branch there, and the two men, almost exact contemporaries, became lifelong friends. Mr and Mrs Lugt were to put together one of the most fascinating collections of the next 60 years. They were amateurs in the 18th century sense of the word. They amassed shells, English portrait miniatures, Indian miniatures, blue and white china and artists' letters with the same degree of expertise with which they collected pictures, drawings and prints. Mr Lugt died on Rembrandt's birthday, and was, like the artist, a Mennonite. He seemed austere and I never saw him with a hair out of place, or a button undone, but he had a healthy Dutch appetite. After lunching with General de Gaulle his diary recorded, 'uninteresting pictures, dull guests and no second helpings.' At our first meeting I was nervous, remembering the glacial formality of a visit to Berenson at I Tatti, but they order things differently in the Rue de Lille. He greeted me with scrupulous courtesy and a welcoming smile. During a two hour tour of his collection he imparted endless information. He was then in his late 70s, but I think he only sat down once. It was an unforgettable Master Class. When I thanked him he said "Please come again. We always have time for people who like to use their eyes." I walked home on

MR AND MRS FRITS LUGT

air across the Esplanade des Invalides and bored everyone with his parting words for weeks afterwards.

After the War the Earl of Caledon, who was living in Ireland, asked us to store the pictures from his Hertfordshire house, Tyttenhanger, while he decided what to do about them. They included arguably the most important Dutch mannerist portrait still in private hands, Maerten van Heemskerck's *Lady with a Spindle*. This lady and her companions provided the libretto for a charming annual comedy which ran for nearly as long as 'The Mousetrap'. Once a year Colin would receive a letter from Ireland - I found one recently - "I really must do something about those wretched pictures of mine which you are so kindly storing. I am coming over for Christmas shopping, and wondered if you would come to lunch with me to discuss them". Colin would set out with our up-to-date valuation for the Heemskerck in case a sale might be imminent. He would return at about three o'clock, his always healthy complexion a shade rosier than usual, murmuring, "The food really is very good at White's". "But Colin," we

would cry, "what about the pictures?" "Well, do you know", he would answer as he adjusted the fire-screen in the board-room, "somehow he never got around to mentioning them and I didn't like to bring the matter up". These two old friends, who originally met in the First World War, contrived to play out this happy autumnal ritual until the Earl died in 1968, and it was only after Colin too had retired that we eventually sold the Heemskerck to Baron Thyssen.

Sir Ralph Richardson rarely missed our Watercolour Exhibitions. His favourite artist was John Varley. He usually arrived on a powerful motor bicycle - a B.M.W. I am told. Once he brought another famous theatrical knight on the pillion. It was fascinating to hear, as they removed their crash-helmets, the beautifully modulated tones of the greatest Hamlet of our century enunciate the words "Ralph, dear boy, you really do drive *much* too fast".

Richardson's enthusiasm made his visits great fun, but he could be brusque. When I said how much I had enjoyed his performance in the title role in 'Uncle Vanya' he snorted, "Oh, did you. I could not understand the fellow at all myself," and stumped away. Fine clocks were another of his many passions. Asked by his doctor if he had recovered from 'flu he said that he was fine but

THE EARL OF CALEDON

SIR RALPH RICHARDSON
Courtesy of the Hulton Picture Company

No such Pirandellian doubts as to the nature of reality arose with another theatrical visitor who was unashamedly acting all the time.

Sir Campbell Mitchell-Cotts had sufficient private means to do what he enjoyed most, which was to play small parts on the London stage. His professional colleagues regarded him tolerantly as a genial amateur, but seeing him recently in the television replay of an old film, I was impressed by the clarity of his diction which must have been welcome to old or deaf playgoers. In Agnew's he played two rôles. For Old Master Exhibitions he acted the Connoisseur of the Old School, a man with a natural eye for quality; for contemporary shows he was the enlightened Maecenas, a fellow who could recognise talent when he saw it and liked to help it along. Monocle screwed in position, and trailing behind him a Pekinese called Daisy, he would silence all other conversation in the Gallery with his powerfully voiced comments. In a Christmas Present Exhibition - drawings under £10 in those days - he bought a couple and presented them, one each, to two other clients who happened to be there. The first, presumably brought up never to accept presents from strangers, refused the gift, whereupon the other, a man of a more pragmatic turn of mind, said he would take both and disappeared into

SIR CAMPBELL MITCHELL-COTTS

one of the clocks was going badly, and would the doctor come and have a look at it as soon as it was possible. For our generation he was incomparable in two parts - Falstaff and Bottom the Weaver. I noticed that when particularly struck by a drawing, his features would assume the same look of wide-eyed amazement that they had done in the latter rôle when Bottom wakes from his dream and begins the speech, "I have had a most rare vision..." Was it, I wondered, his natural reaction to something extraordinary, and did he therefore use it on the stage, or was he simply acting and registering what he thought was the appropriate emotion under the circumstances? I doubt if he knew himself.

Bond Street with them under his arm before anyone could object. This open-handed generosity was typical of Campbell. When he bought a picture, whoever went to hang it was liberally rewarded, and junior salesmen were often invited to lunch on the spur of the moment. Food rationing was still in force and junior salesmen were not overpaid - they still aren't - so these lunches, often at the Savoy Grill, were very popular.

Shakespeare must have known someone very like Ralph Edwards when he put Fluellen into *Henry V*. If Ralph came in on St. David's Day, I would have hidden to avoid being forced to eat a raw leek as was poor ancient Pistol in that play. At all other times Evelyn and I rushed out to meet him if we heard that he was in the Gallery, so stimulating was his company. We were told that a recurrent illness had made him in his earlier days an abrasive and difficult colleague but when we knew him, the right pill had been found and the former angrily flashing eye and rasping voice of which people spoke had mellowed to a genial twinkle and an infectious chuckle. There lurked in his character, as with all the best Welshmen, an element of Dylan Thomas' 'No Good Boyo' and his conversation was designed to provoke, particularly in political matters about which he felt strongly. His knowledge of English furniture was legendary, but he had too a sharp eye for pictures. Appropriately, he was one of the first to appreciate the work of Richard Wilson's fellow countryman and contemporary, Thomas Jones. Long before the rest of us, Ralph had recognised the quality of those intimate *plein air* sketches of Welsh valleys and sunlit Neapolitan walls, today so sought after and so expensive. When his book *Early Conversation Pictures* appeared Evelyn took what Henry James would have called 'the rash and insensate step' of saying that he was enjoying it. "How far have you got?", asked Ralph with a look of deep suspicion. Evelyn

MR RALPH EDWARDS

admitted to only having read one chapter. "Ah", snorted the author triumphantly, "then you still have another 160 pages of closely-packed erudition to come". He was a well-read man, admiring especially the mystic poetry of Henry Vaughan, the 'Silurist' who came from the Brecon country of the Black Mountains where he himself had a house. It was said of Vaughan that he was 'esteemed by scholars, an ingenious person, but proud and humorous'. It could have been said of Ralph too.

If Ralph Edwards personified the Principality, Professor Thomas Bodkin represented John Bull's other island. Shaw's epithet is inevitable for someone who resembled the Irish playwright so closely. The beard, the flashing blue eye, the love of paradox and the witty after-dinner speeches delivered in the soft brogue of the Abbey Theatre, all these were - perhaps deliberately - Shavian. Bodkin claimed that when practising as a lawyer he had gained acquittal for a client accused of murder, which is easy to believe given the fluency of his oratory. The latter found another outlet in a television panel game called, 'Animal, Mineral or Vegetable', whose host was Sir Mortimer Wheeler. When these two men were in form, conversation crackled in a way it rarely does in such quizzes today.

PROFESSOR THOMAS BODKIN
Courtesy of the National Gallery of Ireland

After eight years in the National Gallery of Ireland, Bodkin was appointed as the first Director of Birmingham University's recently founded Barber Institute of Fine Arts. In Dublin he had been frustrated by lack of funds, but he now found himself in the enviable and unusual position of having quite a large sum of money with which to buy pictures for a British institution. Some of his purchases have been criticised, but the Institute was not opened until 1939 and many were made in wartime. When the National Gallery and all other museums were closed, a buyer had to rely on his eye and memory with no other way to check other pictures for comparison with something that he was considering. Remembering this, it is remarkable how good many of his acquisitions were.

Bodkin was an old friend of Sir Alfred Munnings, with whom he shared an intense hatred of Picasso. The Spaniard inspired some of his highest flights of invective. One might feel that he took pleasure in having such a target for his richly worded tirades, but on the last occasion that Evelyn and I saw him, we realised how really deeply he could feel about things. He had always wanted a great Claude for the Institute and in the year of his retirement the wonderful landscape from the Ashburnham Collection appeared in Sotheby's. He must have felt that it would make the perfect final acquisition on his part for the collection which he had built up. Alas, he was outbid. We agreed that we had never seen a look of greater sadness on a man's face as he left the saleroom. Ironically, the successful bidder was Mr E.E. Cook, who subsequently donated the picture to Birmingham's other museum, the City Art Gallery.

Paul Wallraf had a wonderful eye, widely ranging tastes and the acquisitive instinct of a magpie. He could rarely resist buying anything he liked even though he had nowhere to put it. Descended from Ferdinand Franz Wallraf, who

with Johann Richardt had founded Cologne's great museum, Paul lived in what was for post-War days a sizeable apartment with large rooms. They soon proved to be far too small to contain his collection. Visits, though immensely enjoyable, had elements of both the obstacle race and the assault course. There was simply nowhere to put down one's drink or, eventually, anywhere to sit. Objects of all kinds occupied every inch of space and the walls were so thickly hung with pictures that smaller drawings lay flat or propped against their neighbours. Just when it seemed he would be evicted by his collection, the flat immediately above became available, so he took it and started collecting all over again. Then *Lebensraum* became available in Venice in the '60s, when he took on the first floor of the Palazzo Malpiero Trevisani in Campo Santa Maria Formosa. Shortly after Paul acquired this Venetian outpost Carlo Bestegui died and a sale of his collection was held in the Palazzo Labia. The Italian Government, concerned that the better things should remain in Italy, were delighted to hear that many of them only made the journey by canal from the Cannaregio to the *piano nobile* of the Palazzo Malpiero.

Paul made a very happy marriage with Muriel Ezra, the widow of a distinguished zoologist, who built up his own private menagerie in Surrey in the days before safari parks proliferated in the English countryside. Pre-War south-bound motorists may still remember, soon after leaving the Kingston by-pass, being stared at by supercilious llamas and ruminant bison from a field on the left which was the boundary of the Ezra estate. Marriage gave a new thrust to Paul's collection. He now bought figures of animals and birds in every conceivable medium from bronze and terracotta to ivory and jade. (Sotheby's entitled a section of his posthumous sale catalogue 'The Wallraf Menagerie'.)

Paul and Muriel entertained lavishly and were much loved in Venice. Every morning throughout the summer they would march smartly from their *cabana* at the Albergo Excelsior to the Hotel des Bains at the other end of the Lido. There they would touch the boundary fence and march smartly back again. This daily parade assumed for the *bagnini* something of the significance that the Changing of the Guard has for London's tourist guides. From the Regatta to the Fireworks, Venice has always laid on regular spectacles for her visitors, and here was a new one.

MR AND MRS WALLRAF AMONGST THEIR COLLECTION

EPILOGUE

I REMEMBER TWO PARCELS. THE FIRST WAS discovered unattended on the pouffe during a period of intense I.R.A. activity, so we cleared that end of the building and alerted the police. They arrived simultaneously with another visitor who said "I bought some coffee at Fortnum's earlier today. I wonder if I could have left it here when I went round your exhibition?" This incident obviously occurred in variant form all over London, but our other parcel was of a more surrealist nature. It consisted of a sponge bag, containing a face flannel and a slice of turbot, and was left, with some frames, by Duncan Grant who said that he would collect it later, but never did so. The weather was warm, and as we had no refrigerator in those days, we telephoned to Charleston for instructions. Clive Bell, who answered, said that Duncan had gone to France that afternoon for a few days and suggested that we destroy the turbot. He thought, however, that Duncan would like the sponge bag back, so we put it in a safe with the frames, where it was rediscovered during stock taking the following January.

Writing about the Bloomsbury Group has become a growth industry, and I can only add a brief postscript. In 1960 Sir Geoffrey Keynes, an old friend of Colin Agnew whom he had known at King's, asked my uncle if he would come down to Sussex to check the condition and insurance valuation of the collection of pictures formed by Maynard Keynes. On the economist's death these had passed to his widow, the prima ballerina Lydia Lopokova, who retained a life interest pending their eventual bequest to King's College. Colin, who disliked making valuations, and did not share the growing enthusiasm for Post-Impressionism, suggested that I should go instead. In the train to Lewes, Sir Geoffrey warned me that like

Vanessa Bell CARTOON OF LYDIA AND MAYNARD KEYNES
by kind permission of the Provost and Scholars of King's College, Cambridge

other old people who have lived long in a foreign country, Lopokova had days when she reverted to her native language. Even if this were one of them, he added, conversation would not be difficult at lunch as Duncan Grant and Vanessa and Clive Bell, who all hated being out of things, would be there and the real difficulty would be getting a word in edgeways. It turned out not to be one of the dancer's Russian-speaking days, although it would not be strictly accurate to say that she spoke English.

She was tiny, and never sat still for a moment. When I arrived she was clearly expecting Colin, because she darted across the room on the tips of her toes as she must have done 40 years earlier as the Doll in *La Boutique Fantasque*, grasped me with both hands and said "Oh my good God, you are so, too tall to be an Agnew!" Lunch was hilarious, everyone talking at once, no-one listening, and a great deal of laughter. Conversation spurted off in all directions, and I longed for a tape-recorder, but sadly only two fragments remain in my memory. Roy Harrod had recently completed his biography of Maynard Keynes, and had asked his widow what the economist most regretted not having achieved in his lifetime. "I tell him," she said, "if Maynard live again, he drink ever so much more champagne!" In the middle of a fascinating discussion about Derain's wartime activities, she suddenly gripped my arm and fixing me with a fierce look said, "Never, no never, will I allow that Charles Morgan to my house again!" Clive spluttered with laughter and said, "But you can't say that Lydia, because he's never been here before!" And Duncan Grant added with a stutter, "And anyway, I believe he's dead." The dancer released my arm, poured herself some cider, and cried triumphantly, "So you see, always I am right!"

The inter-relationships of the Bloomsbury Group have confused and maddened the outside world and much of what they thought and wrote has failed to stand the test of time, but my dominant impression of its last four survivors was of the enormous fun they seemed to generate. When Berenson coined the phrase 'life enhancing', he certainly did not have Bloomsbury in mind, but that afternoon it struck me as the right epithet for them.

DICK KINGZETT

I am most grateful to all those who helped me find the photographs used to illustrate this article.